DISCIPLING
LIKE THE MASTER

About the cover: *Discipling Like the Master*'s theme of following Jesus' example to make disciples is echoed from page to cover. The cover artwork captures a visual story of Christian discipleship; with a colourful textured pattern and intricate outline displaying times of bright clarity filled with forward movement and breakthrough, alongside periods of dullness. Living the Christian life is complex and varied. The figures walk together through this unpredictable landscape; young and old, from all nations, leading, following or offering teaching hands, and ministering to one another as they seek to follow the footsteps of the Master.

DISCIPLING
LIKE THE MASTER

The Development and Practice of a Christ-like
Ministry of Disciple-making in the Church Today.

STEPHEN J. TURNER

Discipling Like the Master
Published by Stephen James Turner
with Castle Publishing Ltd
New Zealand

© 2023 Stephen James Turner

ISBN 978-0-473-68081-7 (Softcover)
ISBN 978-0-473-68082-4 (ePUB)
ISBN 978-0-473-68083-1 (Kindle)

Editing:
Sally Webster

Production & Typesetting:
Andrew Killick
Castle Publishing Services
www.castlepublishing.co.nz

Cover Design:
Cathy Turner
with Michael Howard

Scriptures are taken from
The Holy Bible, English Standard Version®,
copyright © 2001 by Crossway Bibles,
a publishing ministry of Good News Publishers.
Used by permission. All rights reserved.

ALL RIGHTS RESERVED

No part of this publication may be reproduced,
stored in a retrieval system, or transmitted
in any form or by any means, electronic, mechanical,
photocopying, recording or otherwise,
without prior written permission from the author.

In memory of LeRoy Eims

Jesus said, 'Follow me, and I will make you fishers of men.'
(Matthew 4:19)

*Jesus said, 'Go therefore and make disciples of all nations,
baptising them in the name of the Father and of the Son
and of the Holy Spirit, teaching them to observe
all that I have commanded you.'*
(Matthew 28:19,20)

Foreword

This book is a keeper. Its value comes as a real testimony to the how and why of biblical discipleship. I've known the author for many years; and now he writes as one retired from pastoral leadership. That's one of this book's values: it's not just theory. It's a review of a pastor who early learned the vision and practice of Christian discipleship from LeRoy Eims of the Navigators. And the fruit of his ministry is seen not only in New Zealand, but also in India, where he poured his life and vision over the years into scores of pastors-in-the-making.

So my testimony regarding this author and his text is that he spells out the process for making disciples, and it's all within the Church. That's one of the insights – and perhaps the most valuable – of this volume. Discipleship is the task of the Church! Stephen spells out what that means. And his own life and ministry bear witness to this vision. I'm thankful he has taken the time to share it. This should be a great encouragement to pastors, as well as lay persons.

Kenneth G. Smith, Pastor (Retired)
Reformed Presbyterian Church of North America

Contents

Introduction	13
Part 1. How Did Jesus Train His Twelve Disciples?	19
1. He Called Them to Be with Him	21
2. He Called Them to His Words	29
3. He Called Them Each by Name	35
Part 2. How Does Jesus Train His Disciples Today?	47
4. He Calls Them Through the Testimony of His People	49
5. He Trains Them Within the Church	57
Part 3. Practical Insights into Disciple-Making	67
6. As Loved Apprentices in the Church	69
7. The Disciple-Maker's Goals for the Disciple	83
8. Examples of Disciple-Making	93
Closing Cadenza: A Meditation on Themes of Disciple-Making	103
Notes	111
Resources	115
About the Author	116

Introduction

I enrolled in seminary only days after my twentieth birthday, and very soon afterwards began to wonder, 'What does a pastor actually do?' In answer to that question, I was led to two outstanding men.

One day, in the second aisle of the seminary's library, I 'met' the great 19th-century English preacher C.H. Spurgeon. I think it was in the third volume of one of those collections of extraordinary sermons he had preached in London when he was still in his teens and early twenties. I opened the book at random, and read only a single page before realising that I had found something that spoke to my deep need of forgiveness.

Spurgeon's theology gave me hope, and filled my heart with something big and solid, to say the least! He made me want to be an evangelical preacher of the Gospel, like he had been.

Then, in my first years in the ministry, I met the second man, LeRoy Eims. At the time he was Director of US Ministries for The Navigators, an organisation started by Dawson Trotman prior to the Second World War, for the purpose of reviving the principle and importance of Christian discipleship, and building into Christian living and ministry an emphasis on disciple-making. I was fascinated.

At one of his conferences I asked him to teach me how to make disciples. He agreed unhesitatingly and, over the following three days, gave me many hours of his time. I had not experienced such warmth and generosity in a Christian leader before. But, more importantly, he gave me the answer to a key part of the question that had worried me as a theological student: What was I going to be doing as a pastor besides preaching and visiting the congregation? He opened my heart to what I might be – a pastor who was also a disciple-maker.

I had found two of the most precious things any pastor could ever wish for: a *theology* for a Gospel ministry in Spurgeon, and a *method* of Gospel ministry in Eims.

I am indebted to a number of people, particularly those in my family, who have loved me over the years. But I feel especially indebted to these two men, who have left an indelible mark on my heart and life.

I have never found Christian ministry easy. On many occasions I have wanted to give up being a pastor. There were times when I came near to hating it. I'm sure there are those who would not consider me a 'success' if they were to review my life's work. However, I can truthfully say that throughout the past fifty years of ministry, challenging as they have been, I have essentially remained true to what these two men taught me – the theology I discovered in my youth, when I first read Spurgeon in the library, and the method of ministry I learned through LeRoy Eims, who gave me so much of his time and love at that conference years ago.

On leaving seminary I chose to accept a call from a small group of believers to be their pastor. They had determined to close their church within a year, should my ministry have no effect and the church not grow. My task was essentially a restarting of the church, and God met me in that challenge in such a way that the church grew wonderfully. Then, after further academic study, I was sent to plant a church in another city, and there I remained for thirty years. During that time I visited India, Sri Lanka and Kenya; in the case of India, about twenty-five times, working with young men who for the most part were studying for the Christian ministry. After leaving this second church I was sent to plant yet another church – where I am presently an elder and am mentoring two young men, both of whom have recently been appointed as our pastors.

I'm a dairy farmer's son, which probably explains why I chose to live in the countryside on the outskirts of my city. There I enjoyed the wide-open spaces, and had a big garden with no near neighbours! It was peaceful, and was the greatest place to bring up our seven children.

Our 'section' was once part of a dairy farm. We started our garden from scratch – initially there was nothing on our land but grass and a heap of loose soil left over after building the house. Setting up a garden is a serious business; you don't just rush into making it. You first have to envisage shapes and forms, perspective and colours. And, very importantly, you need to plant for your children. People definitely don't plant this way if they're planning to move on in a year or two. They'd probably plant nothing new! Or they would go for the cheap option of fast-growing shrubs and annuals, for immediate effect. I did the opposite. I planted nyssas, maples, beech and hornbeam – all slow-growing trees. For the most part, the plants I love take a lot of work. I like roses, but they're very time-consuming in our climate. However, the results are worth all the work! After twenty-four years the garden was starting to look beautiful, especially in the spring and autumn.

The Church can learn much about ministry from this approach – that good things take hard work and generally take a long time to come about. And therein lies the problem, for who likes slow development in ministry or relishes a lack of immediate results? Not many of us! Who likes small beginnings, small congregations and hidden-away ministries? A well-known New Zealand author spoke to that very question when he said in regard to ministry in the Church, *'Not everyone is willing to sponsor a minority cause.'*[1] That's so true! Who keeps working at evangelism when, day after day, even month after month, one sees little or no interest on the part of the person they're investing so much time in? Who appreciates practising a way of ministry that for the most part goes unnoticed? Who likes staying in one ordinary place that little bit longer so as to be able to put in the time necessary for growth? Not many people!

People are impatient. They like success that's just around the corner. They prefer taking the easy path to the top of the mountain.

But here's the thing: if Jesus were suddenly to arrive at your church today, what would He think of what is being done, how it's being done, and why it's being done? What would He think of the things your leaders believe are most important in Christian ministry and spend most of their time working towards fulfilling? *This book addresses one particular question – what would Jesus think of the way your church cares for those people who, by his grace, have come to believe the Gospel?*

I've already cited two verses from the Gospel according to Matthew. One can think of these two verses as forming bookends to his account of the ministry of Jesus. In other words, the subject of disciple-making begins and ends Matthew's account of Jesus' earthly ministry. Why is this? Because it defines both the ministry of Jesus, as well as the expectations He has for His people.

The first bookend is Matthew 4:19: *'Follow me, and I will make you fishers of men.'* In this verse Jesus commands those He called to 'follow' Him and promises that He will 'make' them into 'fishers of men'. A transformation of life and direction was promised, simply through their being with Him. In later years those who observed these disciples associated their striking abilities and way of life with their having been with Jesus (Acts 4:13).

The second bookend is Matthew 28:19,20: *'Go therefore and*

make disciples of all nations, baptising them in the name of the Father and of the Son and of the Holy Spirit, teaching them to observe all that I have commanded you...' Here Jesus commissions His disciples to 'go' and 'make disciples', and explains how that should be done. These commands in Matthew 28 are backed on either side by two remarkable claims Christ makes concerning Himself: *'All authority in heaven and on earth has been given to me'* (Matthew 28:18), and *'behold, I am with you always, to the end of the age'* (Matthew 28:20). They highlight His extraordinary, continuous and absolute authority, as well as His everlasting presence with His people. When taken together, they form the greatest possible basis for the confidence, peace and comfort that these eleven disciples would enjoy when embarking on His mission to 'all nations' in the power of the Holy Spirit, whom they were soon to receive.

This great command was originally given to the 'eleven disciples', known as the apostles. But this perhaps leaves some with the question: Can these words be rightly applied to His people today? In answer to this I believe that the Church has no alternative but to say 'yes', arguing that if those great assurances of His power and presence remain true, as they do, then so too must this command (which is embedded in those claims) remain true for the Church today. In addition, it can be argued that the Church's mission cannot be any other than the very same mission which the apostles were given – because Christ remains the Saviour of the world, people continue to need His forgiveness and His disciples in every age will go on needing to learn to obey Him.

This command has not changed, nor has it been withdrawn! Of course it cannot be changed, for we read: *'Forever, O LORD, your word is firmly fixed in the heavens'* (Psalm 119:89). None of the apostles was exempt from this final command. And none in today's Church ought to feel he or she is exempt either. The Lord continues to call *all* of His people to follow Him. He continues to call the *whole* Church to make disciples. And He continues to make those disciples who follow him into 'fishers of men'. Christ's commands stand true today, and this same Christ continues to live and work in His Church.[2]

I am therefore arguing that disciple-making ought to be considered normative within the Church today.

In the first section of this book we will be looking at how Jesus trained His twelve disciples by calling them to Himself and to His words. In the second section we will consider how He trains his disciples today, calling them to faith in Himself and to obedience to His words (within the context of His people, the Church). The third section is practical, with attention being given to the disciple's imitation of others' lives and faith. We will look at the disciple-maker's goals, and then at a series of examples from my own recent disciple-making. In the fourth and final section, Jesus' words in John 12:24 form the basis for my concluding remarks.

PART 1

HOW DID JESUS TRAIN HIS TWELVE DISCIPLES?

The four Gospel accounts of Matthew, Mark, Luke and John are, to my mind, the very heart of the Bible. If you picture a stone landing in a pond and sending out ripples, then these four Gospel accounts are where the stone lands in the Bible. Here we find the greatest point of impact – God's revelation of Himself in Jesus Christ.

If you are a person who knows nothing about the Bible, I'd recommend that you begin reading right there. And when you have finished reading these four books, I'd suggest that you read them all over again! In the following pages you will see that I refer very often to them, as in these four Gospel accounts you will learn how Jesus trained His twelve disciples.

CHAPTER 1

He Called Them to Be with Him

We should begin by asking the question: Why did Jesus invest so much time in so few people? After all, He had a number of people following him, yet in the beginning of His ministry He *'called His disciples and chose from them twelve, whom he named apostles'* (Luke 6:13). Why did He do that? Many people have asked this question, because they probably thought, 'How foolish. If I had been in that situation, I would have done things differently. Twelve men are not much of a foundation if He was intending to establish a universal Church!'

These reservations are easily dispelled by looking at the four Gospel books. Jesus did it this way because there was nothing He wanted more for those twelve men than that they should be 'with him'. *'And he appointed twelve (whom he also named apostles) so that they might be with him...'* (Mark 3:14). This would not have been a feasible option were fifty people to have been called, whereas twelve could be 'with Him', close to Him and aware of everything to do with their Master.

Right at the very outset of His ministry, He called these few men. He called them because He had chosen them. Look at the lovely invitation He gave to two of John the Baptist's disciples the day after His own baptism. They had asked Jesus, *'Where are you staying?'* He replied, *'Come and you will see'* (John 1:38,39). John's disciples were so struck by this invitation that years later they could remember the exact hour it was given, and how their lives with Him had begun (John 1:39).

The power of their subsequent witness, their testimony, was founded on their having been with Him and having seen His glory with their own eyes (John 1:14). Because they had been with Him they could testify to having heard Him, to having seen Him with their own eyes, and to having touched the Word of Life with their own hands (1 John 1:1-4).

It was their personal, physical association with Christ that gave their written testimony its watertight credibility, so that the Apostle John was able to say in his own written account: *'we know that his testimony is true'* (John 21:24). The Gospel accounts are eyewitness testimony, as are the remaining Scriptures, for Jesus says of the latter, *'it is they that bear testimony about me'* (John 5:39). We dishonour the apostles and, more importantly, we dishonour Jesus Himself when we reject their words as being untrue.

Why else did Jesus choose to have twelve men with Him? His aim throughout His ministry on earth was, at least in part, to replicate Himself in the lives of these men. To do this He had to have them 'with Him'. They were called to His side, to be His disciples.

It has been suggested that perhaps the nearest equivalent to 'disciple' is 'apprentice'. An apprentice learns by watching what is done by the 'master', be that person a builder, a plumber or whatever. The apprentice plumber learns under the watchful eye of the master plumber. By choosing these men, Jesus Himself exemplified how to make disciples. And, all importantly, He underscored the importance He attached to disciple-making, through His own commitment to them and to their development.

Jesus wanted them to see in Him what it was to be truly a *'fisher of men'* (Matthew 4:19). He invested His life in theirs so that, in seeing Him, they would learn how to become 'fishers' too. There is no other more important thing that emerges from being an apprentice to Christ than this – that they be trained to be a fisher of others.

> *What is the object of being apprenticed to a builder but to learn to build? What is the outcome of being joined to a Saviour if we do not learn to save? Though we might ourselves be saved, should we be His disciples indeed?* [1]

These are the words of the great missionary to China, Hudson Taylor, in about 1886.

The English preacher C.H. Spurgeon obviously had this same idea of the multiplication of Gospel ministry on his mind when he made the following comment about a famous 16th-century Christian leader.

> *How much have other nations derived from the little republic of Switzerland on account of Calvin's having the clear common-sense to perceive that one man could not hope to affect a whole nation except by multiplying himself, and spreading his views by writing them upon the fleshy tablets of the hearts of young and earnest men!* [2]

Spurgeon clearly admired Calvin for thinking this way, for Spurgeon too longed to multiply the same ministry of the Gospel that he lived for. So, in 1855, when he was just twenty-one years old, he established a college in England for the training of preachers. He too believed that this could best be done by gathering together men under his leadership. Like Calvin, Spurgeon was a disciple-maker.

A later example of this love of a multiplying ministry may be found in the life of Dietrich Bonhoeffer. He is usually admired for his truly memorable books, two of which, to my mind, are outstanding – *The Cost of Discipleship* and *Life Together*. His immense character is everywhere in his writings. However, perhaps the greatest thing about this extraordinary man who lived in Germany through the Nazi terrors of the Second World War was the fact that he gave himself and his life to a few handfuls of young men. He met with them in the underground seminaries in the 'sandy Baltic outposts' of Finkenwalde in Pomerania and in Zingst. Then, when all seemed lost, he met with them in the 'collective pastorates', which were small, hidden gatherings of young men preparing for Christian ministry in the hope of better days to come.

Bonhoeffer was disenchanted with the theological instruction offered in the universities and, given the circumstances of the time, had no option to do other than what he did. He believed that the study of theology and the training of men for the ministry was best undertaken within an atmosphere of worship and silent meditation, and in singing, playing and eating together. Most importantly, this was carried out under the supervision of his loving companionship. To my mind, Bonhoeffer, more than anything else was a disciple-maker.[3]

There is no doubt, however, that the Lord Jesus is the master disciple-maker. None can compare with Him. But how was He to replicate Himself in human beings other than by first becoming a human being Himself? The book of Hebrews simply says, *'Since therefore the children share in flesh and blood, he himself likewise partook of the same things'* (Hebrews 2:14). So Jesus was born as a baby. He was once a youth. He was obedient to His parents. But there is added another layer – He took the *'form of a servant, being born in the likeness of men'* and *'he humbled himself by becoming obedient to the point of death, even death on a cross'* (Philippians 2:7-8). He was truly with us in our humanity – in our lives, in our sufferings, and in our temptations. Jesus was pre-eminently a servant. He exemplified that greatness of humility before His men. John 13:1-20 gives us insight into His servant heart.

However there can be no doubt that, central to an understanding of Jesus' servant-heartedness and His humility, is the cross itself. There is no way of understanding Jesus other than by addressing the subject of the cross. He made the cross the critical component for a right understanding of His life and ministry. The cross epitomised the essence of His life. He became a human being for the very reason of going to the cross. He came to die. He appointed twelve men to be 'with him' so that they might see with their own eyes the Servant and Lord of Glory lay down His life for His people – for their sins – on that cross.

Mark 8:31 tells us: *'And he began to teach them that the Son of Man must suffer many things and be rejected by the elders and the chief priests and the scribes and be killed, and after three days rise again.'* From Mark 8:34 onwards Jesus swiftly brings all of His disciples into the very orbit of the cross. He describes Christian discipleship as having self-denial at its heart – the taking up of one's cross and following Him along those same paths of suffering and humiliation.

As Bonhoeffer famously said, *'When Christ calls a man, he bids him come and die.'*[4] There is no other biblical form of Christian living or of Christian discipleship. There is no other form of Christian ministry. In the words of Hudson Taylor in 1889, when speaking at the China Inland Mission Conference about their intended work in China: *'This work will not be done without crucifixion, without consecration that is prepared at any cost to carry out the Master's command.'*[5] These are the clear words of one who deeply understood the nature of true Christian ministry and discipleship.

This truth of Jesus' unique servanthood, of His embracing the cross and thereby laying down His life for His disciples, is *the* key component when considering the subject of disciple-making.

Jesus was The Servant and, as such, this was His chosen way of shaping the thinking of His disciples and making them into the men He wanted them to be. They were *with* this Servant – they were with their Lord and Teacher, who washed their feet as a slave would. This same Servant was the Master who would teach them how to fish for men. So when His disciples take up the cross like He did, and endure sufferings for righteousness' sake, and give up their lives for Him, they are adopting His way of discipling and discipleship.

It's through our taking up His cross that we come to be like Him and, being like Him, we long to seek and find those who are 'lost', as He did. It is through our trust in the message of the cross, and in teaching the same, that other people are brought to know the true Christ – as opposed to a false Christ who is ashamed of the cross. Nothing could be more important to the disciple than the cross, for as Paul the Apostle says it is by faith that His people are united to Him in His death. We are 'crucified with Christ'. It is in following the crucified Lord that we 'crucify' our sinful nature in a world now 'crucified' to us (Galatians 2:20, 5:24, 6:14).

This same crucified Lord is the great disciple-maker, and it is this great fact that must be at the heart of our quest to become disciple-makers today.

The making of a Christian disciple-maker then begins and continues and ends here – with Christ in His servant-hood of the cross. It begins with a call to follow this crucified Jesus. The disciple's first steps, and all those steps that follow, are to be in the steps of this crucified One. Here, in the company of the crucified Christ, the disciple hears His words, walks with Him, watches His every interaction with people, and is in closest emotional fellowship with Him (1 John 1:1-4).

As the crucified Lord of Glory, Jesus has every right to command our deepest love and service. The cross overwhelms our hearts in a torrent of compelling love. We owe Him everything! He now has complete right of ownership over us. He can demand our all, even our physical death – and especially the death of our sins, even our most cherished ones. It must be said that nothing of what we give to Him can ever put Him in our debt. '*I never made a sacrifice*',[6] wrote Hudson Taylor, that famous 19th-century pioneer missionary to China, in recognition of Christ's absolute right over all he was and all he possessed. Our 'sacrifices' are not sacrifices at all, but rather His dues; '*...we have only done what was our duty*' (Luke 17:10). Like the man in this parable, we will only sit down when Jesus directs us to do so, and we will serve until that moment.

The apostles were called to be 'with Him'. This being so, what can we say about the relationship between the disciple and his fellow Christian disciple-maker? Namely this, that the disciple-maker should not want to be the object of the love of the person he is discipling. He should want that disciple to be the Lord's disciple and not his own.

Jesus, of all men, Himself being God, can unashamedly call on His chosen ones to love Him. Dietrich Bonhoeffer underscores the absolute exclusivity of love for Christ in discipleship when he says, '*Jesus Christ stands between the lover and the others he loves.*'[7] That is to say, Jesus will not have any human being, be he or she a deeply respected disciple-maker or not, stand in His way and get in between Himself and His disciple. Another human being may *well* be worthy of great respect and love. That might (and indeed ought to be!) an effect of his or her Christian ministry. But it should never be the desired goal. '*I dare not,*' says Bonhoeffer, '*desire direct fellowship with them.*'[8]

Jesus is the end-goal. Jesus alone is to be truly and deeply loved. The Twelve were called to be 'with Him', and He had every right to ask it of them, since to love and obey Jesus was to simply obey the Law that they love the Lord their God with all their heart, soul, mind and strength (Mark 12:30). Jesus is Lord and, as such, jealously desires, and has every right to receive, the love of His own.

With that in mind, let me ask this question: What was behind Jesus' calling these men to Himself? Was it because He wished to use them as part of His overall strategy to conquer the world? There's no denying that they were His instruments in bringing the Gospel to people yet unsaved (John 17:20), but to presume that this satisfactorily answers the question in full would be incorrect.

Jesus called these men to be with Him because He loved them, and because He knew that to be with Him was the most precious experience any human being could ever enjoy. He called them to Himself so as to love them, and He '...*loved them to the end*' (John 13:1). No one loves as Jesus loves. Jesus alone is the 'lover of my soul', as the 18th-century evangelist Charles Wesley says in his famous hymn, 'Jesus, lover of my soul, let me to Your presence fly'. The twelve apostles were called to Him in love, for love. They were called to be 'with Him' that they might see and receive His wonderful love for them and in return give their love to Him.

Can there ever be a happier place on earth for any human being than in the love of our Lord and God? And to be with Him in Paradise is where He wants us all to be. Jesus will take His people to Himself, to be loved for all eternity (Luke 23:43, John 14:3, Jude 21).

CHAPTER 2

He Called Them to His Words

The disciple-maker is in some ways like a ghost-writer: he does not want his own 'voice' to be heard. He wants Christ's words to be the only voice listened to by the person he disciples. This will be the case when the disciple-maker follows the method of the Master himself.

Jesus makes it clear in John 10:1-18 that His people will 'hear His voice'. Their hearing of His voice identifies them as His people. It is this fact, above all others, that distinguishes His people from those people in the world, who may listen to the Gospel and yet not hear His voice. This is true of all His people in every age and place – that they hear His words and know His voice. They are able to do this because the Lord first knew *them*, and called them by name (John 10:3).

The disciple-maker is looking for and is able to help that person (and only that person) who hears the voice of Christ – because only such a person, who loves the 'voice' of Christ (and therefore also His words), will want to obey everything Jesus commands him or her to do. This disciple's obedience to His Word is the most identifiable sign that he or she loves Him (John 14:21).

Jesus came to public attention through preaching the Word of the Gospel. His ministry commenced with His preaching. Matthew says, *'From that time Jesus began to preach...'* (Matthew 4:17); that is, from the outset of His ministry He preached the Gospel of God.

Matthew then goes on to record what those first words were: '*...Repent, for the kingdom of heaven is at hand...*' (Matthew 3:2). These same words are recorded in Mark's Gospel: '*Now after John was arrested, Jesus came into Galilee, proclaiming the gospel of God, and saying, "The time is fulfilled, and the kingdom of God is at hand; repent and believe in the gospel"*' (Mark 1:14,15). This preaching of the Gospel of repentance for the forgiveness of sins was the essential central element in Jesus' spoken ministry. He was a man of words, and His words were '*...the gospel of Jesus Christ, the Son of God*' (Mark 1:1). He is called '*...the Word...*' (John 1:1).

Jesus underscored the inseparability of Himself and His words. In his *Institutes of the Christian Religion*, John Calvin says something beautiful about this inseparability, and about our reception of both Christ and His words when we believe – '*This, then, is the true knowledge of Christ, if we receive him as he is offered by the Father: namely, clothed with his gospel.*'[1]

In coming to Christ, we come to His Gospel words. Take, for example, the following teaching of Jesus: '*...If you abide in me, and my words abide in you...*' (John 15:7). He doesn't say 'and I abide in you', as the reader might expect (although that too is true for the believer). Rather Jesus says that *our abiding in Him* is perfectly balanced by *His words abiding in us*.

This same close association of Jesus with His words also appears in Luke's Gospel: '*For whoever is ashamed of me and of my words...*' (Luke 9:26). Christ did not ever want to be considered apart from His words. Indeed, the true Christ *cannot* be considered apart from His words. When a person comes to Jesus, he or she comes into the presence of His words that are to be received and obeyed. A true disciple-maker will always lead new believers to Christ's words.

The Lord stresses the importance of His words for several reasons. Firstly, He says they are His Father's words and, as such, not

His own: *'For I have not spoken on my own authority, but the Father who sent me has himself given me a commandment – what to say and what to speak'* (John 12:49); *'For I have given them the words that you gave me...'* (John 17:8); *'I have given them your word...'* (John 17:14).

His Father's words were the most precious thing Jesus could give to His disciples. A most profound respect and love for His Father's words were at the heart of His commitment to teaching them to His disciples. He gave the Father's words to His disciples, and they are, unsurprisingly, 'spirit and life' in the hearts and minds of believers today (John 6:63).

Jesus did not reject Peter's confession, when he said to his Master, *'Lord, to whom shall we go? You have the words of eternal life'* (John 6:68). This was true – Jesus alone had the words of life, and there was no one else to turn to. Another layer of authority was therefore added.

The words of Jesus had immense importance – not only because they were the Father's words, but because they had become the Son's own words too. The Son's authority is clear: *'Everyone then who hears these words of mine and does them will be like a wise man who built his house on the rock'* (Matthew 7:24). Again, *'The one who rejects me and does not receive my words has a judge'* (John 12:48). And yet again, *'Whoever does not love me does not keep my words...'* (John 14:24). Christ Himself is the very source of these words, and as such they are to be respected and obeyed by the Christian disciple. Our Lord Jesus' words were given to be obeyed, not merely believed.

This is especially relevant to us in the light of our subject of disciple-making. Jesus says that they were to teach disciples *'...to observe all that I have commanded you...'* (Matthew 28:20). It doesn't say that they merely ought to be 'believed', but rather that they be 'observed' (or obeyed). Undoubtedly, to rightly believe His words is to obey them. The life of the disciple is a life of living, ongoing obedience, a life of submission to Christ's words. The emphasis is on obedience, and it is a necessary and noticeable one. His disciples are saved that they might obey.

The 'obedience of faith' referred to in Romans 1:5 and Romans 16:26 highlights the Apostle Paul's understanding of the nature of true faith. Obedience to Jesus Christ is God's ultimate purpose in saving His people (1 Peter 1:2). Sadly, that emphasis is not always apparent in the message the Church brings to the world, and even to its own congregations! Discipleship doesn't consist merely in the enjoyment of fellowship, in pleasure of Gospel music, in expressions of spiritual fervour, or even in further and further opportunities for studying the faith. The disciple-maker's goal is the disciple's obedience to Jesus Christ. It does not matter who that disciple may be. One may be a highly-intelligent young pastor; another may be someone who holds an important position in business; another may be a mother at home with little children. No matter who they are or what they do, the goal remains the same: obedience to Jesus' words.

All too often that goal can be lost sight of in disciple-making. The disciple-maker may get irritated when his instructions are ignored, or when an appointment is forgotten, or when his plans are not enacted on by the one he's endeavouring to help. When this happens the disciple-maker is in danger of making his own words and his own demands pre-eminent, and his own authority paramount. The goal for the disciple-maker needs to remain clear: he is there to help this new Christian hear, understand and obey Jesus' words.

The benefits of obedience are overwhelming. Jesus says: *'If anyone loves me, he will keep my word, and my Father will love him, and we will come to him and make our home with him. Whoever does not love me does not keep my words...'* (John 14:23,24). These words of Jesus conclusively link His presence to our obedience to His words and as such they guard against an unanchored emotionalism; warm, intense feelings which produce no personal or moral commitment to obey His commands.

Jesus commits Himself to be present with every disciple who obeys His words in love. Here each is enjoying the other – the disciple enjoying Jesus by flinging open his heart to become a home for his Master's words; and the Lord, in turn, enjoying the disciple who obeys Him, loving His disciple in a super act of grace. This, for us, is to 'glorify' and 'enjoy' Him. To love Christ in this way is our 'chief end', as the answer to the first question of the famous *Westminster Shorter Catechism* tells us.

Our words may sometimes have a comforting quality to them, but all too often they are sharp, rude and divisive. When the latter happens, people move away and keep their distance from the speaker. No one wants to be in the presence of destructive words. But Jesus' words are *never* like that; they build people up! When they are believed and obeyed, they build a most wonderful thing – a home. This is the very image Jesus uses: '*If anyone loves me, he will keep my word, and my Father will love him, and we will come to him and make our home with him*' (John 14:23).

Nothing else quite summons up such happy scenes as does the word 'home'. However, I am painfully aware that for many people this is simply not true, and that many of them are traumatised and bitter because of their homes. This is because it's universally believed that home is equated with trust, love, comfort and peace. Sadly not for them. *But there is hope!* Christ creates, in increasing measure, the blessing of a *true* home in the hearts of those men, women and children who commit themselves to obeying His words. As each of them welcomes in Jesus' words, inviting them into his or her heart, Jesus himself is welcomed in and comes into the warmth of that love!

I had a happy home because my parents were disciples of Jesus and honoured His words. Not until my teenage years was this peace disturbed, and illness led to words being spoken that still hurt when I think of them today. *Jesus' words*, on the other hand, always bring sweetness and light to the believer; when welcomed in, they become a home-maker, and our harassed and troubled hearts are transformed into a place of peace and rest. Only Jesus and His words, when received as a welcome guest, can create in the heart such a home. Then the believer, together with God the Father, God the Son and God the Holy Spirit, will sit together around our 'table' with Gospel truth as their love's joy. There is no home like this anywhere on this earth, for where else could one find such a gathering of the true God and a human being?

CHAPTER 3

He Called Them Each by Name

Have you ever wished that you could have been there in Galilee with Jesus and those privileged disciples? In 2016 my brother and his wife went to Israel, and walked beside that very lake, right where Jesus once had been. I guess the lake itself, as well as the surrounding countryside, is essentially the same now as it was way back then. I've so often wished that I could have been there with Him. Why do I feel this way? One reason in particular comes to mind. Our hearts are made for companionship, and as Christians our hearts are made for *His* companionship in particular. Jesus became a human being – not only to be our Saviour, but also because He wanted to let His disciples see, in His humanity and in the proximity of His companionship, just what extravagance of love was in store for all of them. This love would be given not only those apostles who were with Him in Galilee, but also all those disciples who would follow later.

Could it be that an all-too-frequent absence of companionship in the Church today makes that ache for His companionship more intense? Believers long for the companionship of fellow believers. I believe that loving, personal and caring companionship, centred around confession of sin and prayer, is one of the most desperate needs of the Church in the West today. From my experience of working with people in India for twenty-five years, together with my life-long knowledge of the Church in New Zealand, I believe that there is a desperate need for the experience of real love between fellow believers everywhere. People are starving for the love of someone who will love their souls.

Jesus is the outstanding Lover of the soul. We need His love more than the love of any other. No other companionship, be it in the Church or outside it (marriage included) can fill the void in the human heart that cries out for love; and that is as it should be. The Psalmist says: *'And there is nothing on earth that I desire besides you'* (Psalm 73:25). Jesus knows this, and this is why we see Him devoting His time to loving His disciples individually. In doing so He shows us how disciple-making ought to be done today.

Following are five windows that shine a light on Jesus' relationship with one of His disciples, and which highlight the individuality of His love for each of them. Each window connects us with a moment in time when Peter became the focus of Jesus' attention and, in being such, the recipient of priceless words that touched his heart deeply.

Luke 5:1-11 – The call

Perhaps Jesus' earliest encounter with Peter is to be found in John 1:35-42, but in Luke 5 we have the continuation of that initial contact. Here in Luke's account we read about Peter's call to a kind of fishing that was different to all his previous experience. This takes place on the shores of Lake Galilee, where Jesus was ministering the Word to the ordinary people crowding around Him. He had moved from preaching in the synagogue (Luke 4:16) to doing so on the lake shore, but His word was the same in both instances. Jesus' interaction with Peter begins with asking him to put out his boat a little from the shore.

This passage tells of two miracles – the extraordinary catch of actual fish from the lake, and the greater miracle of the promised 'catch' of men. Both miracles followed Peter's obedience to Jesus' words; in both instances he is asked to obey the Master. As one who knows the Bible would expect, this obedience of faith preceded the miracles. In this regard, consider the words the Master later said to Martha: *'Did I not tell you that if you believed you would see the glory of God?'* (John 11:40)

In the first instance, in Luke 5:4-6 we read that Peter obeys Jesus' word – when he lets down the nets and they secure a catch of fish the size of which they'd never seen before. In the second instance, in Luke 5:10-11 Peter obeys Jesus' word of promise, and leaves behind everything to follow Him. Jesus surrounds His commands to obey and believe with promises of great reward. And so Peter goes on to 'catch men'. Just read the first few pages of the book of Acts, and you'll see I'm correct in saying that the Lord honours our faith with blessing.

Peter has already lent his boat as a preaching platform, and now he obeys Jesus' command and sets out to fish again, after a hard and joyless night which produced nothing. This time the result is incredible. Peter is overwhelmed: *'Depart from me, for I am a sinful man, O Lord'* (Luke 5:8). Such a display of power made him rightly afraid of Christ, for in His presence he was acutely aware of his own deep sinfulness. It's in this context that his training as a believer begins. The miracle of this great catch of fish, and Peter's subsequent sense of horror in the presence of such power, form the foundation of Jesus' call to him to a greater work than fishing on a lake. Jesus' command, when believed, and the subsequent first miracle, encouraged in Peter a confidence of faith needed for the realisation of the second miracle – fishing for men.

John 21 – Jesus' call reissued

When we read John 21, three previous events in Peter's life come to mind: the miraculous things that took place earlier on the same lake (Luke 5), a different meal in a different place, which ended with Peter's loud professions of faithfulness (John 13) and, lastly, the events around Jesus' arrest – Peter's cowardice, his denial of Christ, his lies and his public unfaithfulness (John 18). All of these resonate in the mind of the reader when reading this chapter.

Three years had passed since Peter first met Jesus (John 1:40-42). Over the course of these years he had seen the glory of Christ (John 1:14), His suffering and crucifixion and, on two subsequent occasions, His living presence after His death. Notwithstanding this, Peter had returned to old, familiar places and the former ways of his working life as a fisherman, and probably of his childhood. He was presumably seeking comfort and rest for his shattered spirit. Yet we see that he was not able to find rest even in these familiar things, though his soul longed for it.

This is when Jesus appears for the third time. A typical night's fishing ended only in emptiness and frustration. John 21 says that *'they caught nothing'*. It's then, in that night of failure, that we again see that same kind of miracle as performed in Luke 5 following Peter's obedience. We see the same kind of vehemence too – when he confesses his sinfulness. Here Peter throws himself into the water in his desperation to be with Christ again, to find reconciliation and rest for his deeply troubled heart, after the calamity of his deserting Jesus on the night he was betrayed. Here is Peter thirsting for Christ's forgiveness.

We read in John 21:15-25 how they walk along the beach together. Jesus asks Peter whether it is indeed true that he loves Him more than 'these'? (To my mind, 'these' are the other disciples, and their love for Christ). Peter's earlier, shockingly public denial of Christ had brought the disciple down to their level; he now no longer can claim a deeper love for Jesus than they do. No, says Peter, he doesn't love Jesus more than they do, but he does know that he loves the Lord! And it is his unshakable conviction that Jesus knows that too.

Peter's response is so modest – there is no longer any pride, anger, irritability or bragging; not even expressed shame. All he can do is quietly appeal to Christ's thorough knowledge of him, and wait on Christ to deliver a verdict. Peter has no stomach now for making any self-assertions. He rather looks to the Master. *'O Lord, my heart is not lifted up; my eyes are not raised too high... but I have calmed and quieted my soul, like a weaned child with its mother...'* (Psalm 131:1,2). Here we witness the silence of a soul that wants the love of Jesus. What peace Peter found that morning on the shores of Galilee!

Why is this such an important moment in Peter's life? Because there is no way any person can serve Christ's people and be useful to the Master without owning his or her own weaknesses and sin. Human strength will always fail. Jesus clearly shows us here that strength for Christian ministry is made perfect in the knowledge of our weakness.

The Lord's original call to Peter is then reissued – because he is now ready to take it up. A *'broken and contrite heart'* (Psalm 51:17) is the required state necessary for doing Jesus' will. Nothing less will do. Now 'shepherding' replaces the 'fishing' of Luke 5. 'Catching' is replaced by 'feeding', and his ministry is now clearly portrayed as the giving of himself to others with the compassionate, caring love that is born of a repentant and forgiven heart.

His life's work, his future, is clear. Now Peter wishes to know what would become of 'the disciple whom Jesus loved'. What would his future be? His curiosity meets with a sharp rebuke from the master trainer: *'If it is my will that he remain until I come, what is that to you? You follow me!'* (John 21:22) As J. Oswald Chambers has written,

> *Jesus wants heroes, not busybodies... He allows Peter to smart under the rebuke. He does not even correct his mistaken assumption that John would not die.'* [1]

The Gospel of John's account of Jesus' ministry to His disciples begins (in John 1:39,43) and ends (in John 21:19,22) with these same words of command to Peter: 'follow me'. This is a fitting conclusion to Peter's training. This is his future. This encapsulates the heart of Christ's teaching on discipleship.

Matthew 14 – Walking on the water

In Matthew 14:22 Jesus sends His disciples off by themselves. Why did He do that? Was this by mistake? Did He do it to detach them from a dangerous popular trend that was looking to make Him king (John 6:15)? Did He want to be alone? Or did He do it perhaps because He wanted these men to know something more about trusting in Him? The last option seems the most likely one to me.

Jesus had purposefully placed these men in circumstances beyond their control, at a time when He was not physically there with them and able to help them. And they evidently had no expectations of His being able to help them. He was too far away. Darkness only accentuated their feelings of utter helplessness as they sat in their boat in the middle of the Sea of Galilee. Alone with their unbelief, they could make no progress that night in the midst of the violent storm that raged around them.

In Mark 6:48 we read that Jesus 'saw' them. Even though He was on the mountainside and they were on the lake with the night surrounding them, He knew their situation. They thought they were alone, far offshore, but He saw them straining at the oars. Nothing is a barrier to the love of Christ for His people, be it distance, darkness or terror.

'When you pass through the waters, I will be with you' (Isaiah 43:2). This is never more wonderfully true than when He sends His people out into the world to make disciples. Often they are far from family, friends and the gathered Church, and in cultures and places where they encounter only contempt or threatening silence. *'But*

immediately Jesus spoke to them, saying, "Take heart; it is I. Do not be afraid"' (Matthew 14:27). These words are a bedrock for creating a living faith in Christ.

The second lesson that Jesus taught His men is that so much can be achieved through faith. More than we can imagine. This lesson was one that especially involved Peter. Initially he is astonished at Jesus' walking on the water, and for a moment the disciple obeys the word of Christ, gets down out of the boat and walks on water himself. But then he sees the wind, and he becomes afraid and starts to sink. Now there's a story for Peter to tell his grandchildren! Jesus' immediate rebuke was that Peter was a man of 'little faith' who doubted his Saviour's word. Had he trusted in Christ, he might have walked on water! Here Jesus is calling for a living faith, as He does throughout the Gospel accounts, and Peter is reminded that such a faith will be stupendously blessed.

Jesus' commands and the promises at their core to those who believe continue to amaze us today. *'For truly, I say to you, if you have faith like a grain of mustard seed, you will say to this mountain, "Move from here to there", and it will move, and nothing will be impossible for you"'* (Matthew 17:20-21). And again, *'Truly, I say to you, if you have faith and do not doubt, you will not only do what has been done to the fig tree, but even if you say to this mountain, "Be taken up and thrown into the sea," it will happen. And whatever you ask in prayer, you will receive, if you have faith'* (Matthew 21:21-22).

These promises are considered too fantastic for church-going people in the Western world today. They're so great that they leave the average Christian teacher nonplussed as to how to explain them. However, the quest for this living faith must be at the heart of Christian discipleship because it honours the Master, who gave us such extraordinary promises. It takes Jesus at His word. He never promised nonsense. He is always to be believed.

Mark 8:31-38 – The crucifixion

Little words are never unimportant in the Bible. Look at this verse: *'And He began to teach them that the Son of Man must suffer many things and be rejected... and be killed, and after three days rise again'* (Mark 8:31). The seemingly unimportant word 'and' commences this sentence. It's there in the text to indicate to the reader that something had happened beforehand – something that had evidently provoked Jesus to make the remarks that followed. That 'something' seems to have been Peter's insightful confession: *'You are the Christ'* (Mark 8:29). But how could that ever have been an issue for Jesus? Surely Peter was correct? Jesus, however, knows how ignorant people are. They did not properly understand the true Christ, and it's evident from His remark in Mark 8:32 that He considered Peter to be one of those who did not fully understand Him. Peter needed divine help to understand the Christ, and the Lord gave him that help right there (Mark 8:31).

Jesus' teaching on the Christ would have been shockingly at variance with popular opinion. He spoke 'plainly', so that there could be no misunderstanding on this subject closest to His heart.

The Christ, He said, would suffer, be rejected and die at the hands of the religious leaders. He gives details of this event in Mark 10:33,34. Christ's death was a necessity. He 'must' suffer, He 'must' be killed – but not because He was caught up in their hatred or swept along on a tide of jealousy that was too powerful for Him to resist (John 19:11), but rather because it was the Father's will that He die (Acts 2:23, 4:28, Isaiah 53:10). *'No one takes it from me,'* Jesus said, when speaking of His life (John 10:18). Mark says that He gave His life *'as a ransom for many'* (Mark 10:45).

Jesus is compelled to defend this portrait of the Christ. Peter is so inspired at one moment, and then is so horribly misled the next, for Jesus' understanding of the Christ did not sit happily with his own. Peter robustly denounces what he believes to be

Jesus' appalling misrepresentation of the Christ. But if Peter's words are vehement, Jesus' are more so. He turned and looked at His apostles before answering, so that they would all clearly hear His uncompromising reply. *'But turning and seeing his disciples, he rebuked Peter and said, "Get behind me, Satan! For you are not setting your mind on the things of God, but on the things of man"'* (Mark 8:33). Do we ever read words like these in the Gospel accounts and wonder at them? Some might consider Jesus' statement to be overly harsh. But Peter's words and his reasoning endangered God's people, and Jesus' response is more like the snarl of a mother bear protecting her cubs. His people were threatened by Peter's rebuke of Him, a rebuke so deep, so dark, and so horribly uninformed, that the Lord lashes out as He does, with these words. Too much was at stake to leave it unchallenged.

Behind Peter's rebuke was a lie that did not in any way reflect the mind of God, but bore all the marks of Satan, who plots to erode the Lord's plan of redemption. The glory of Christ is effectively lost when the cross is in any sense avoided or diminished by the Church. Christ without the cross, in any culture or age, will not do. An un-crucified Christ is a christ from hell, an impostor, and needs to be put firmly out of the Church at any time and in any place. The Church has nothing worth preaching and nothing worth hearing when Christ is not preached as crucified (1 Corinthians 2:2).

All this gives us a wonderful insight as to how Jesus trained His twelve apostles. He was prepared to defend the truth with the sharpest, most public and personal rebuke if that was necessary. Nothing less than the truth would suffice, and His disciples were to operate within this truth of the crucified Christ.

But Jesus is not finished with the subject of His suffering yet. His disciples too would suffer and die like Him. The same sense of necessity in regard to Christ's death, evident in Mark 8:31, applies to the disciples: '*...let him deny himself and take up his cross and follow me*' (Matthew 16:24). They were to '*...share his sufferings*' (Philippians 3:10), '*...filling up what is lacking in Christ's afflictions...*' (Colossians 1:24). While there is certainly no suggestion here that Jesus did not sufficiently die for our sins, Paul is making the point that Christ's sufferings continue today in the sense that His disciples throughout history will suffer for His cause. They will be reviled and persecuted because they love the Lord Jesus.

No other form of Christian discipleship is presented to the reader of the New Testament – Jesus carried His cross and was obedient to the point of death (Philippians 2:8), and so when we walk in Jesus' footsteps we too come to the cross. 'Follow me,' says Jesus, and leads His disciples to the cross. They do not have any other path offered to them. Christian discipleship begins at the cross and continues with the cross, because the disciple is 'in Christ'.

Such a picture of Christian discipleship is not attractive to me! I dislike pain, and cherish being accepted. I don't like being jeered at in public when I speak of Jesus. However, such distaste fails to recognise the truthfulness of one great fact – that we live in a world that hates the Master and consequently will hate those who love Him (John 15:18). Before my wife and I visited Italy a few years ago, the picture I had of the Cinque Terra was one of blue skies, warm ramblings and sunny slopes. However, the reality was cold rain, grey seas and squelch. So too, Jesus' comments on the cost of Christian discipleship need to be taken as the absolute truth.

Martin Luther makes some insightful remarks about this association of Jesus and His disciples in death:

> *On the Cross he was utterly alone, surrounded by evildoers and mockers... So the Christian, too, belongs not in the seclusion of a cloistered life but in the thick of foes. There is his commission, his work. The kingdom is to be in the midst of your enemies. And*

he who will not suffer this does not want to be of the Kingdom of Christ; he wants to be among friends, to sit among roses and lilies, not with the bad people but devout people. ²

A true disciple knows where he ought to be. It is not in a place of comfort and warm acceptance, but out among those who need a Saviour, where derision and rejection of Christ are commonplace. That's where He was when on earth. That's where the disciple is to be.

Mark 10:17-31 – Always in His debt

The wealthy man in this passage fascinates me. He's confident in his obedience, and yet so dissatisfied. It took a direct hit at his wealth to uncover the reason for his deep unhappiness.

This man asked a question that couldn't be bettered. However, the fact that no one could be saved by trying to be good had escaped him. Jesus said it was 'impossible' for any man – be he rich, poor, or even aspiring to be good – to be saved apart from the power of God, with whom everything is possible, even the salvation of the privileged class, to which this man belonged.

Peter's response to that revelation was to remind the Lord Jesus that they had been good. They had done exactly what He had advised the rich man to do. They had 'left everything', fishing businesses and lucrative tax offices included, to follow Him. Was Peter merely comparing himself favourably with the rich man, or was he expressing his alarm that there might be no reward at the end of all their sacrifice? Jesus replies to Peter's self-confident claim by saying that the rewards for discipleship were beyond anything he could contemplate, and were to be enjoyed 'now in this time' (Mark 10:29,30).

This is an extraordinary promise to His disciples. I can't think of any other promise quite like it. Jesus does not intend to ever be in our debt. Our indebtedness to Him only grows as our discipleship continues. This promise is to every disciple of Christ's, including those who might be tempted in times of cruel persecution to wonder whether it has all been worthwhile, and to those who might be tempted when facing pointless failure in Christian ministry or in their struggle with sin, to feel He has deserted them.

Jesus is never out of reach, never unaware of the commitment and hard work of the disciple (Hebrews 6:10). The disciple gives, but Jesus gives even more back. His gifts to us will more than outweigh any loss we may experience in giving. I've just finished reading a biography on the very remarkable 19th-century missionary to Algeria, Lilias Trotter, who lived out the truth she here asserts: *'It is loss to keep when God says "give".'*[3] Perhaps this was what the wealthy man knew in his heart to be true when he went away 'disheartened'? He had 'lost' the enjoyment of eternal things on earth by 'keeping' his financial assets.

This probably seems startling, and even perhaps ridiculous, to an unbelieving heart. But for millions of suffering Christians who have been separated from their family and deprived of all their possessions for love of Christ, these promises have given them what the world cannot give – His peace, a sense of His presence, and the enjoyment of His loving care here on earth in the very midst of suffering for the Gospel.

At the conclusion of the account, there is a final flourish of a promise to round off all these promises, to comfort the suffering Christian: '*...and in the age to come eternal life*' (Luke 18:30). *What more could a person want?* What more could a person look forward to?

This is Jesus at His most compassionate and most serious. This is Jesus training His disciple Peter for the long road ahead, when Peter would be without His physical company and when, perhaps, he would be without the loving company of family or fellow believers.

PART 2

HOW DOES JESUS TRAIN HIS DISCIPLES TODAY?

When Jesus says, *'Follow me, and I will make you fishers of men'* (Matthew 4:19), He says it to us now. Though Christ is not physically present, He continues to do what He 'began' to do during his earthly ministry (Acts 1:1). He continues to make 'fishers of men'.

My point is that Christ Himself (not the Church) is the true maker of disciples today. He alone is to be 'followed', and He alone makes His followers into 'fishers of men'. He alone is the Lord of the harvest, and the Church therefore needs to do as He commanded by praying to Him to provide the workers that He alone is able to equip.

The Church's finest moments are when its members and leaders gratefully and humbly acknowledge His presence with them, His presence in leading them and His great accomplishments through them as His people.

When we set out to plant our church seven or eight years ago, I was appointed as leader. I was more than willing to lead, but I admit to being afraid. What, I asked, would become of the venture should we not find younger leadership? Would believers come and join us to help form a foundation strong enough to be able to begin financially supporting a full-time ministry? Church-planters are few and far between, and it is probably because too many Church leaders fear the unknown, as I did, and are not prepared to commit to such a venture. Just as most people want to buy a house already built, rather than go through the pressures of building one from scratch, so too most leaders prefer to live in comfortable, settled and established church communities.

Clearly the Church must have more builders, if new churches are to be established. Yet, when all is said that can be said about the workers, it remains forever true that only Christ can build the Church. He's the true church-planter; He's the disciple-maker; He's the one who grows the Church by adding to it those He saves.

How are believers discipled today? The same way they always have been – the Lord Jesus disciples them. So then the question is, how does the Lord train His disciples today?

CHAPTER 4

He Calls Them Through the Testimony of His People

The disciple-maker's life begins with his being brought to Jesus. The Church (that is, the people of God) are those through whom His Gospel comes. People are brought to Jesus through the words of other believers, as they bring His Word to them.

The testimony of others
Very occasionally a person comes to Jesus and receives His Word without the involvement of anybody else. Sometimes, usually in places where the Scriptures are not easily procurable, a person may be led to the Word by way of a dream. However, more often than not, when a person comes to Jesus, they come with the help of another human being. That helper is very often not the public preacher. Take Philip, for example. He was not an apostle. He was appointed to 'serve tables'. He was directed to a desert road, where he found an Ethiopian traveller and '...*told him the good news about Jesus*' (Acts 8:35).

These tellers of the Gospel story were often nameless ordinary folk who, though driven out of their homes by persecution and difficulties, 'preached the word' wherever they went, as in Acts 8:4.[1] We read in Mark 5 the account of a man who was extraordinarily transformed by Christ, and who went on to become a classic example of ordinary folk telling other ordinary folk about the Master (Mark 5:19).

People bring the Word. The Apostle Paul sums up the nature of his own ministry in these terms: *'For I will not venture to speak of anything except what Christ has accomplished through me to bring the Gentiles to obedience – by word and deed...'* (Romans 15:18,19). While the supernatural element is rightly kept to the fore, the human element, however, is not lost sight of.

If you would like other great biblical examples of how the Lord uses others to bring us to Him, just take a look at the first chapter of the Gospel of John. Look at the place personal testimonies play in bringing others to Jesus, as in this account of what happened on the day immediately following Jesus' baptism. Firstly, John the Baptist directs two of his disciples to Jesus through his words, '...*Behold, the Lamb of God!*' (John 1:36) Then read what Andrew (one of the two) did as his first act as a brand-new disciple of Jesus. The first thing Andrew did was to find his brother Simon and tell him, '"*We have found the Messiah" (which means Christ). He brought him to Jesus*' (John 1:41,42). In the following verse, Jesus finds Philip and then Philip 'found' Nathaniel, and said, '...*We have found him of whom Moses in the Law and also the prophets wrote...*' (John 1:45).

I think it's fascinating that this is John's account of the opening day of the ministry of Jesus, who came into this world to save sinners. The training of these apostles in disciple-making began with Jesus inviting them into His home, where He spoke to them and spent the day with them. Those whom Jesus had sought out in love then immediately (and not surprisingly) took on the role of evangelists from the very outset of their discipleship, and in so doing imitated their Master's most outstanding feature. Just as He was a 'fisher', so they, too, instinctively became 'fishers' as soon as they came to know Him.

Those people were brought to Jesus by their friends. They were brought through the persuasive words of personal testimony. In his commentary on the Gospel of John, D.A. Carson comes to this wonderful conclusion when speaking on the 'foundational principle' of Christian expansion through the centuries: '...*new followers of Jesus bear witness of him to others, who in turn become disciples and repeat the process.*' [2]

The shape of Christian testimony

I love classical music. When I'm on a device, most of the time I'm listening to classical music. I'd have given a lot to have gone to the Proms in London's Royal Albert Hall in 1997 to hear the astonishingly gifted pianist Evgeny Kissin (and all those encores thrown in!). When I sit at my piano these days and the family are here, I often have a little grandchild on my lap for a music lesson. I want them to love music too. At the moment, they are mostly hearing Chopin's Nocturne, Opus 55, No.1.

A genuinely saved believer is always mad-keen to introduce others to Jesus – Jesus has saved him or her from sin, and the believer now loves Him completely and wants others to meet the Saviour. The Christian prays for these opportunities to speak about Jesus. He or she looks for them, searches for them, whether at work or on the beach or in a camp-ground. He or she listens for them.

Nearly every circumstance potentially throws up an opportunity for a lover of Jesus to talk about Him, because it's easy to talk about someone you love. One doesn't need written notes, because it's all written on the heart; nor prep time, because one's life has been lived with Jesus up to that point. When one is weak in living with Jesus, abiding in Him as Jesus says in John 15, then opportunities are not recognised. The heart, and consequently the mouth, have nothing much to say about Him.

Can I tell you of one such opportunity I had a few years back? I was standing on what surely must be one of the most magnificent beaches in the world – Whale Bay, in Northland, New Zealand. It was a summer's day, and the sea was the clearest blue-green. A couple who were visitors to New Zealand were in the water, she swimming and he wading up to his knees, and I said something innocuous like 'beautiful, eh?' as he waded past. He stopped and smiled, and paused just long enough for me to continue that conversation he had commenced with his smile. We talked in the water for an hour or so – about Europe, politics, history and touring New Zealand. That took up the first hour, and then we got on to Jesus and, in particular, why I love Him.

Months later that lovely young couple took up my invitation given them on the beach that day, and came to stay with us in our home. They hardly knew us, nor we them. It took some courage on both parts! Some years have passed and I continue to be in touch with them, and as often as not Jesus is referred to.

The disciple-maker is foremost an evangelist, and as such must be able to speak of his or her own love for Jesus, if that conversation is to be persuasive and effective. It is all too evident to the observer when a disciple truly loves Jesus. An ambassador – and Christians are 'ambassadors' (2 Corinthians 5:20) – represents his or her country's interests and emotions regarding the subject that is being addressed, whether before enemies or allies. I say this because as Christian ambassadors we are called on to speak as though God were making His 'appeal' through us (2 Corinthians 5:20). We know from the Gospel accounts just how winning were the ways of the Lord Jesus when He spoke to men and women. The disciple of Jesus needs the emotions of Jesus – gentleness, compassion – and the assurance of one who knows the Father, for God's appeal through us to be effective.

When people think of passion they think of sporting events, or a person's devotion to a charity or music. But all these lack the one ingredient that sets a Christian's passion apart from all other passions: the love of Jesus! This passion, this happiness with Jesus' love and mercy toward us, is deeply important when it comes to evangelism. I have always hated the thought of Jesus as the 'friend of sinners' being represented by me when my heart is unmoved by those who don't know Jesus. Why would anyone whose heart was untouched by the love of Jesus want to speak about Him?

More importantly, why would anyone ever want to listen to some indifferent, bland report about Jesus? As Christian people we ought to desire a genuine passion for Jesus. He deserves nothing less! Otherwise the words we need to say will not be found, the music will fade, and Gospel notes of joy will not burst out of our heart.

The Gospel should never, ever be disassociated from the joy and confidence of having found Him! If none of this joy and assurance is present, then the Gospel is no good news at all to the hearer. Our hearts should be as joyous as those of the folk in Luke 15 who found their precious lost sheep, lost coin and lost son, and who ran off to tell their friends of their great finds!

At the beginning of his book *Evangelicalism Divided*, Iain Murray cites William Tyndale's definition of the Gospel: *'Evangelion (that we call the gospel) is a Greek word; and signifieth good, merry, glad and joyful tidings, that maketh a man's heart glad, and maketh him sing, dance and leap for joy.'* [3] Crucially, Tyndale recognised that there is joy in those who believe the Gospel. Tyndale understood that where there is no joy, no Gospel can have been received.

Testimony that is copied

A baby's first glimpse of the world is likely to be that of its mother. So too the disciple's first glimpse of the Christian world is most likely to be of that person whose life and words led him or her to Jesus, be it through public preaching or personal conversation. The new disciple will consequently be forever grateful to that person who brought the Gospel to him or her.

The new believer will more likely copy that friend than not. In the late 19th century in China a scholar and opium addict named Hsi came to believe in the Gospel through the ministry of David Hill. Hsi then spent two happy months with this missionary. Hsi's biographer comments on his tremendous attachment and admiration for Hill, and his desire to copy him.

> *Perhaps nowhere is the great law of heredity – like father, like son – so clearly seen as in the relationship between the missionary and his spiritual children. They have practically no other standard, and can imagine no higher ideal than the life he lives before them, and unconsciously his example becomes the limit of their expectation and attainment.*[4]

Hsi went on to be a pastor in China, and committed himself to a lifetime of evangelical activity. His life proved beyond doubt the truthfulness of this observation that new believers will most likely copy the one through whom they have come to believe. In light of this observation, how tremendously important it is that the evangelist, the member of the Church who is doing the telling, speaks of the God and Father of our Lord Jesus Christ – the God of the Scriptures!

Gospel testimony and love

The famous American chef and lover of French food, Julia Child, who is portrayed so wonderfully in the movie *Julie and Julia*, apparently said that one can never have enough butter in one's cooking. As a New Zealander and the son of a dairy farmer, that is music to my ears, because butter is very big here!

When one thinks of disciple-making, one can never have enough love – the love of Jesus. From the time I first became a pastor I have always been deeply impressed with the words of 1 Thessalonians

2:7-8. What a summary of his ministry Paul gives us here! And it's taken directly from the life of Jesus the disciple-maker.

Paul and his colleagues 'shared' with the Thessalonians both the Gospel and their 'own selves'; and the latter is to be understood within the context of their having been the most loving carers of the Thessalonian believers. They gave truth, but not only truth. They gave their own lives, with an affection that both loved and longed for the good of those they cared for.

The sharing of the Gospel was to have been expected, for what would their ministry have been worth to any human being, had they not given these Thessalonians this happy news of Jesus? However, the Gospel is not intended to be presented on its own in Christian ministry. It calls for something more than simply the telling of the Gospel that saves. It calls also for the love of the evangelist for Jesus especially, and for those who hear. Paul is therefore not content with sharing the Gospel of God alone. He adds these words, *'not only... but also our own selves'*, lest his readers miss the all-important point that the love of the disciple-maker, who is *'...like a nursing mother taking care of her own children...'* (1 Thessalonians 2:7,8), is as essential an ingredient to successful disciple-making as butter is to outstanding cuisine.

This is a love as Jesus defines it. It is a love primarily for Himself that wells up in a heart that understands how indebted it is to Him for His love, and His saving forgiveness.

In this sense Paul's ministry was exceptional. And, just as few followed his example then, very few follow it now. Paul wrote: *'For though you have countless guides in Christ, you do not have many fathers. For I became your father in Christ Jesus through the gospel'* (1 Corinthians 4:15).

It is a sad reality that in the Church as I know it today, this giving of a double gift of both the Gospel and one's own self is so uncommon. And it seems it has always been so. In a letter to a friend

Discipling Like the Master

in 1836, the Scottish minister Robert M. M'Cheyne addresses the importance of this giving of oneself:

> *Another thing that persuades me to write you… is, that I felt in my own experience the want of having a friend to direct and counsel me… I do not mean that I had no relations and worldly friends, for I had many; but I had no friend who cared for my soul. I had none to direct me to the Saviour.*[5]

The giving of this double gift is imperative in the pursuit of a Christ-like ministry of disciple-making.

I referred previously to Pastor Hsi. After two months together, David Hill left for work elsewhere in China. Hsi wrote,

> *We dwelt together rather more than two months. When Mr. Hill was taking his departure he could not restrain his flowing tears. I, also weeping, accompanied him outside the city to the north of the great bridge, and there we parted. Returning, my heart was straitened as I thought of the people around me in great darkness, like sheep without a shepherd; and I feared it would be extremely difficult to find another pastor like him.*[6]

With love like this in the hearts of its early missionaries, is it surprising that today the Church in China is as great as it is? What a solid foundation! This leads us to the following chapter on training disciples within the Church.

CHAPTER 5

He Trains Them Within the Church

The believer must have God's help to become a disciple-maker. God will equip that person with the necessary desires and skills for His work. Having given His Spirit to every person he saves, God now through His Spirit gives gifts of His choosing to these same people. *'To each is given the manifestation of the Spirit...'* This same Spirit *'... apportions to each one individually as he wills'* (1 Corinthians 12:7,11).

Paul indicates that Christ himself is the Giver. *'But grace was given to each one of us according to the measure of Christ's gift'* (Ephesians 4:7). His gifts vary between individuals. And so, as a consequence, each believer has a different contribution to make for the Gospel, and to disciple-making in particular.

The resurrection of Jesus, therefore, is absolutely crucial to our understanding of Christ's ministry. He is now, as the risen Lord, able to continue His work among His people through His Spirit. And He is still giving gifts to all His people, for the same purposes that He pursued when with His apostles on earth.

It takes a church to raise a disciple

Throughout the ages the people of God have rightly understood the Great Commission in Matthew 28:16-20 to be their clear, single manifesto for ministry. Every member of the Church is called to be engaged in some way in this venture of disciple-making, in accordance with his or her gifting. Together, all these variously-gifted people contribute to the overall success of the Church in pursuing this end. Everything in the way of gifts is given for the achievement of the Lord's one great goal – that we go and make disciples of all nations, baptising them in His name and teaching them to observe His commands.

Not everyone has the same gifts, but everyone in the Church is called to be engaged in the overall endeavour of telling people about Jesus and teaching all believers to observe His words. As people sometimes say, 'it takes a village to raise a child', so it can be said that 'it takes a church to raise a disciple'. Some may open their homes in love to these new brothers and sisters. Some may encourage them in their reading of great books. Some may be wonderful in friendship, and others deeply earnest in conversation. Some may have an immense love for those who as yet do not believe, whilst others may be unusually earnest and faithful in prayer. Some may be able to present the Gospel story simply and clearly. But everyone, together, is in this '...*partnership in the gospel...*' (Philippians 1:5).

The whole Church ought to want to see people saved through repentance and faith, and confessing this in baptism before the Church and the world. The whole Church ought to want to participate in the long-haul task of teaching these newly-saved ones to obey all that Jesus has commanded us to do.

Some members of the Church will be particularly gifted with an ability to win the regard of others, and get alongside them and love them. And, should they come to believe, teach them how to live as Christians in this world. These people will stand out in terms of the disciple-making task. They may become known as 'disciple-makers'. It surely stands to reason that recognised pastors and teachers ought to be among these gifted persons. If the Church cannot see in its leaders a commitment to making disciples, then it has every right to be concerned.

Personal and individual ministry

Disciple-making will only be done when one is committed to real-life, genuine interaction on a personal level. Too much of the contemporary pastor's time today seems to be given to activities within the church that are of a non-personal nature – administrative concerns, hours in the office behind a desk interacting with a computer, and hours on social media. The unbelieving person is being addressed from the office desk, rather than face to face!

Where a love of the individual is lacking in the preacher, even devotion to public preaching of the Gospel tends to be remote and, dare I say it, inadequate and unconvincing. A person with a taste for administration, or a love of reading and public preaching or writing, can remove themselves from real person-to-person life in a church. Don't misunderstand me! The public preaching and teaching of the Scriptures is absolutely necessary, and a major occupation of a true Church. But too often, in conservative, evangelical Christian ministry, the private, personal, heart-to-heart ministry between the pastor-teachers and members of the church is a secondary element, while the public ministry is relied upon for all teaching and evangelism. This, however, should not be the case in a sound church. It seems that in many churches today, personal pastoral work (which is what we're essentially talking about) has almost ceased, just as doctor's home visits have now become a thing of the past.

Church leaders often fail to appreciate that people are often more open, more ready to hear the words of Christ within the informality of their own homes, or in a café, or when they '...*walk by the way*...' (Deuteronomy 6:7) with a Christian friend, than within the confines of a formal meeting. There most definitely needs to be greater attention given to personal, individual ministry of the Word within today's Church, especially by its leaders.

We should think more deeply on the words of Paul: '*I did not shrink from declaring to you anything that was profitable, and teaching you in public and from house to house'*, and *'...remembering that for three years I did not cease night or day to admonish everyone with tears'* (Acts 20:20,31). Informality, private spaces and individual concern – these were features of Paul's ministry. Something comparable is to be found in 1 Thessalonians 2:11-12: *'For you know how, like a father with his children, we exhorted each one of you and encouraged you and charged you to walk in a manner worthy of God...'* Public preaching alone would not have allowed him to do this; something more was needed – something that was not in conflict with public preaching but in sympathy with it. Personal interaction with believers in Ephesus and Thessalonica appears to have been of primary importance in Paul's ministry.

Paul was a preacher, but he clearly had far more than Sunday's sermon in mind when he speaks in Colossians 1:28 of *'...warning everyone and teaching everyone with all wisdom, that we may present everyone mature in Christ.'* One can hear the repetitive drumbeat of emphasis those early Christian leaders gave to the individual believer. The Greek text is clear – the accusative, masculine singular of 'everyone' is repeated for effect, lest we miss Paul's point. Each person, each member of the Church, was the object of his care and of the care of his colleagues. They worked together to present to Christ disciples who were mature. This was no superficial investment! Additionally, notice the present tense of the words 'warning' and 'teaching'. This underlines the continual stream of concern for individual members of Christ's Body. There was no let-up in their personal interaction with those they were discipling.

The words of Paul found in Colossians 1:25 regarding his commission should, to my mind, check any tendency we have to place all our energies and hopes in public preaching. (If only that warning were more to the point here in New Zealand! Preaching the Gospel is a dying element in Church worship in this country.)

These words *'to make the word of God fully known'* have frequently been understood as referring to public preaching alone. But is that limitation warranted? Both the scriptural context, with its emphasis on individual pastoral care, and the actual practice of these men in their ministry suggest it should not be.

All too often these days, the emphasis is on the public ministry of a few – the elders or leaders of the church. It is unarguable that these people are of the utmost importance in regard to the Church's mission. But how are these leaders to operate within the Church? I rather like the blunt words of E.M. Bounds in one of his books on prayer. When speaking of the church leader, whom he calls the 'preacher' (in the Western world that title would, for the most part, be considered entirely inappropriate, if not unwelcome!), he says: *'Preachers are not sermon-makers, but men-makers and saint-makers.'*[1] Bounds puts the emphasis firmly where it should be. The leader's goal in public and private ministry is the well-being of the members of the Body of Christ; that those members might grow to *'know Him and the power of His resurrection'*. This is a far cry from placing the main emphasis on the leader, or the preacher, and his or her abilities. And yet the Church too often focuses on those very matters rather than the hearer. The shape of words, the delivery of the spoken message, fame, influence – these should never be permitted to overshadow the overall goal of Gospel ministry.

It all takes time

I have been in full-time Christian ministry for almost 50 years. I look back with nostalgia at the days when I was in my twenties, preaching and evangelising and meeting friends. Things seemed simpler then, and I felt more sure of myself than I do now.

However, there's one thing I now know for sure, and it's that good men and women in the Church are not the products of some one-day wonder, some quick-fix, some six-week course on discipleship, or a series of seminary lectures.

My wife and I have seven children, and it is clear to us that sons and daughters of character don't just appear. Lovely children and youth don't come out of nowhere. They are not made in a day. It takes the committed attention of both parents working with each child to produce character, and to teach him or her the ways and life and the words of Jesus. This is never done in some artificial way but in the midst of family life and all its mess. Can you imagine what it's like bringing up seven children, as we did, in one house? The mayhem! The daily vacuuming, three daily loads of washing, and all those nappies in the laundry sink (before there were disposables)!

Was it an easy thing that Jesus did in training his twelve disciples? No. Was He sometimes dismayed at their reactions to difficult circumstances or their behaviour toward one another? Yes. Their immaturity was an undeniable fact, until the very end of His ministry! Even after His ascension there were doubts among some and general ignorance of what was expected of them. Jesus' training of the disciples was a work in progress, even as He ascended into heaven.

In the Church today, generally speaking, we are in too much of a rush when we make disciples, or pray, and talk to people about Jesus. But Jesus didn't work this way. There was an unhurried aspect to His ministry. Good things in the lives of His sinful followers took time to achieve.

What He had to work with was not promising, if one looked only at the clay, as it were, and took no notice of the Potter. Clay, in its natural condition, is unprepossessing stuff. When one watches a potter at work one can hardly believe that anything so messy could be fashioned into something beautiful. Think how amazed the watching angels would have been when the Creator made man out of earth – a living being, made 'a little lower than the angels' and 'in the image of God'. And think how amazed those same angels are now when they see His recreating work in us who were once hostile and shameful in our behaviour.

Jesus took three years or so to train His twelve apostles. Apart from the two missions we know He sent them on (Luke 9:1-6 and 10:1-12), He kept His disciples close to Him during the whole of His ministry. His careful instructions as to how they were to approach those missions and His subsequent interest in their report back are a window into His basic methodology. He had them with Him as He travelled, when He preached the Gospel, when He healed, and when He prayed. He had them with Him when He rebuked the Pharisees. He had them with Him when He suffered and prayed in the garden and when He was crucified. Some were present when He was on the cross and spoke to the crowd and the thief. They were with Him after He was raised from the dead, and when He appeared to many of them on several occasions in the weeks that followed. And, finally, they were with Him when He was taken up into heaven.

During all this time He was watching them, listening to their questions, and commenting on their reactions to disappointment, opposition and division. He was observing them, especially in relation to their reactions to His Word.

It all took time. He rebuked and exhorted them, and explained things to them. He fashioned them over time into makers of disciples. The same is true today. Nothing has changed with Jesus. We have the same Lord. His goal remains the same – to make fishers of men. And He is dealing with human nature, which is no different to what it was in the first century.

Just as they did back then, so too today good things take time to develop. Disciple-making is a skill learned over time, over a lifetime. It is a vocation that calls for the kind of patience that does not lose heart through the years, as teacher and pupils struggle with deep-rooted sins, unbelief, pride and an unwillingness to deny themselves.

I remember many family fishing trips on the Manukau Harbour in the North Island of New Zealand when I was a boy – baiting the hooks, waiting patiently for a bite, and often pulling up the anchor in search of a better spot. (Grandpa was never satisfied!) I also remember, as a gardener in my adult years, all those times I've had to replant, dig more deeply the bulbs and seeds, and shift challenging shrubs and trees. Disciple-making is not for the impatient Christian. The true disciple-maker watches like a gardener, and is so happy when he sees or hears of some 'green shoot' of good work in the disciple.

In recently comparing the Greek versions of Mark 1:17 and Matthew 4:19, I noticed something I've never noticed before – both verses are similar in that Jesus says that He will make those who follow Him into fishers of men. But there is one telling difference – Mark *adds* the word 'become': *'Follow me and I will make you become fishers of men'* (Mark 1:17). Is there in that one word, in this context of disciple-making, an added emphasis on the fact that disciple-making takes time and effort? The Master Himself worked over the years with His disciples to make them into disciple-makers.

Keeping the goal of disciple-making before the members

It is not surprising that there is such a marked lack of respect for the Church as an institution in the Western world. People sense that today's Church is a far cry from what it was like in the days of Jesus and His ministry.

We cannot go back to operating like they did in the first days of the Church, even if we wished to; subsequent history makes such a return impossible. However, the Church today, with all its structures, forms of leadership, constitutions and tried-and-tested confessional statements, would be wise to address, in every decade and every culture, the question of the nature of true Christian mission. It needs to constantly ask itself the question: What work did Jesus leave for us as a Church to do for Him today?

This question is lost sight of all too often, muffled by the noise of the Church's organised activities and plans. Countless fads and preoccupations make it difficult to address this question. Being human and sinful, we tend to quickly justify our church practices, and dislike their being challenged. But amid the noise, busyness and administrative activity, there need to be people in the Church who keep the following two questions before the congregation of His people: What are we here to do for Jesus? And are we achieving that goal?

We will answer that first question immediately by quoting Matthew 28:19,20: *'Go therefore and make disciples of all nations, baptising them in the name of the Father and of the Son and of the Holy Spirit, teaching them to observe all that I have commanded you. And behold, I am with you always, to the end of the age.'* How can the Church know if it is making this, His Great Commission, central to its life and practice? To answer that, let's ask a series of questions.

Is a voice heard in prayer meetings asking the Lord of the harvest for labourers to be given to carry out this Great Commission? Are there voices in the foyers, buildings and homes of the Church that courageously speak of the Saviour's purpose for coming into the world 'to seek and to save the lost'? Are there members who have an ear and a heart for those who have newly received Christ? If each individual church is a household, a family, then it consists of 'children' (the immature) as well as adults. As a good family it should care for and set aside time for these 'children'. Does the Church do this? Children are never lost sight of in a loving family. What is the Church doing for the 'children' in the faith, to help them grow in grace?

Discipling Like the Master

    Where are you with all of this in your church? And if you know things are far from where they need to be, what are you doing about it? Whatever you do in challenging God's people (and in particular the leadership), always respect them and approach them constructively, with the intention of building up the Church rather than hurting or destroying it through your criticism.

    The fact is, the Church is slammed by the world enough as it is. We expect that. But if the Church is to be constructive in its criticism of itself, it should avoid destructive words and actions. A true Christian man or woman loves the gathering of the people of God, because His Church is a Household of brothers and sisters. The true Christian will always be a churchman or churchwoman, because he or she is by nature a member among many members of the Body of Christ into which they have been baptised (1 Corinthians 12:12,13).

PART 3

PRACTICAL INSIGHTS INTO DISCIPLE-MAKING

From what I've observed over many years, set programmes and courses in the church or seminary often don't help people truly prepare for ministry.

Such programmes are popular because a structured list of ideas and objectives can be worked through, each box ticked and a qualification achieved. But the spiritual life isn't like that.

Jesus had much to say to a people and leadership who were deeply invested in ancient traditions and much-studied laws. He taught that a formulaic adherence to such things as temple sacrifices and public worship, no matter how beautifully observed and no matter the number of boxes ticked, could never make up for a distant heart (Matthew 15:8).

We can be too easily impressed by measurable achievements and appearances. The truth, however, is that the Lord is the only true assessor of spiritual preparedness and the human heart. He alone has the depth of insight necessary for such a role.

With that in mind, what follows is not a course or a programme. Instead, I have set out for you some general observations that I trust are in keeping with the *heartfelt* ministry of Christ to His disciples, and as such are in keeping with the Scriptures.

CHAPTER 6

As Loved Apprentices in the Church

Written or spoken instructions don't really work for me. I much prefer *seeing* it done. And when it comes to technology, I need to see it done a number of times! Then I need to do it myself, over and over again, before I have any confidence I can carry out the task without the supervision of one of my kids! But, hey, I'm not alone. Plenty of people need to be shown how to do things. Jesus understood this principle when He gathered these men together to make them 'fishers of men'. They were about to see the Master doing the 'fishing'!

When I was a child on holiday over summer at a beautiful place called Little Huia, in the North Island of New Zealand, I used to join a great-uncle of mine on the old wooden wharf that then stood there, and watch him fish. He was kind and patient with his great-nephew. I would watch him put on his tracers, his sinkers and hooks, and l would learn the different knots by watching and copying – which, of course, had been my uncle's intention in asking me to join him.

The leadership of the Church is responsible, among other things, for the development and training of the believers, whom we could liken to apprentices. Taking into account all we've said above about Jesus and His disciples, here are four things I'd do to help them develop.

Invest in their lives

A church's task is to help potential disciple-makers develop. To do that, it needs to invest in their lives. But firstly, how will it recognise these people? Leaders will be tempted to make their choices based on physical appearance, gifts of intellect, apparent leadership abilities and social presence. But leaders must look for other things beyond these potentially distracting aspects.

The leadership needs to look for a love for the God and Father of our Lord Jesus Christ, evidenced by an abiding gratitude to Him and a longing to know Him. They should look for a submissiveness to God's Word revealed in the Scriptures, and the evidence of this in ongoing repentance, and a quest for a greater understanding of His truth. They must look for a love of His mission to the world, to seek and to save the lost, as evidenced by a warm, sincere engagement in the lives of unbelievers and a joyful companionship with those who believe.

Leadership can easily overlook investing in the lives of believers in general and, sadly, those believers who stand out in the Church as 'faithful' (2 Timothy 2:2) to the things described in the previous paragraph. These are the very people who leaders, mindful of the future needs of the Church, ought to be considering! Leaders can be distracted by the ever-pressing need to prepare for preaching – for it's an undeniable fact that preaching's very public and appointed nature makes preparation for this activity demanding and inescapable. They can be distracted by those endless, seemingly random and inescapable demands that come with leading a body of people and lose sight of their training role.

The truth is, this lack of investment in the development of a disciple's character, social skills and understanding of the Gospel is not only shortsighted in terms of preparing for the Church's future, but also uncaring in terms of the brother or sister's development.

Sadly, leaders often do not invest in the lives of believers because they are not actually convinced that their time or energy will be well spent in such personal investment. But true Christian ministry is only balanced and healthy when there is an investment in both prayer and public preaching, and teaching as well as direct, personal investment in people's lives.

What is at issue here is the worth of the individual believer – his or her value to the Church and to the cause of the Gospel.

In our church we are about to commence an internship for a young man who shows promise of an earnest willingness to learn, serve and give his life to God's people. People like him are of considerable value to the Church, and rare finds in our country. A church would be foolish to ignore such a person. Both our young pastor and I (as an elder) will be meeting with him every week for the next two years, God willing. In those hours together he will listen to reviews of his work, discuss theological and pastoral issues, and hear me talk about disciple-making and ministry in general and preaching in particular. He will be encouraged to trust in the Lord Jesus with regard to the Gospel ministry he's about to enter into, and to evidence that trust in a life of prayer. He will be told by me, repeatedly, that in my opinion a true Gospel ministry should never waver from a commitment to personal evangelism and personal input into disciple-making. He will work at all these matters while at the same time continuing his theological studies through a seminary as an extra-mural student. He will learn within the church. He will learn the same way as the young pastor, our first intern, has been learning over these past few years.

When a church values a ministry like that of disciple-making (and by implication values her people), the heavy investment of her resources into people is not difficult. I very much like what John Bunyan says, in his book on prayer, about such a spiritual investment:

> *If a man should see a pearl worth a hundred pounds lie in a ditch, yet if he understands not the value of it, he would lightly pass it by: but if he once gets the knowledge of it, he would venture up to the neck for it. So it is with souls concerning the things of God.*[1]

If you believe that disciple-making is valuable to the Church, then you will venture 'up to your neck' for its realisation and practice. Remember Jesus' parables of the treasure in Matthew 13 that not only teach us the comparative value of different treasures but also the sacrifice that the finder needed to make in order to possess the more valuable treasure. Every believer deserves the investment of the Church's resources. Some believers warrant the particular investment of a leader's time and guidance, and a wise leader will gladly give it, despite the sacrifices he must make to do so.

Encourage them in ministry

I remember the first sermon I ever preached. I was twenty at the time, and I spoke on Abraham's servant and his remarkable faith in his quest for a wife for Isaac. At the time I was unmarried, had barely entered seminary, and had never preached in my life before. How wonderful it was to be given that opportunity by a small congregation in the city of Auckland. No one complained after church, although I don't recall any compliments either. I'm rather glad I haven't kept the manuscript! My being asked to preach was all part of my training in that first year. It was a tremendous opportunity to learn, but it had little of the hands-on mentoring that would truly have benefited a beginner. This scenario is all too common in the Church and seminary – a far cry from the ministry of Jesus, who appointed those disciples to be 'with Him', and a far cry from that of Paul, who followed the lead of the Master in this regard. If you're interested, why not search all Paul's letters and the Book of Acts and note how many other disciples were found in his company.

I love the story of C.H. Spurgeon and his first sermon in 1851, when he was sixteen. A Mr James Vinter asked him to go to a village outside Cambridge in England to hear the sermon of a young man whom he said had little experience in preaching. It was a 'cunningly devised' invitation, says Spurgeon in his autobiography. On the way there, in conversation with Mr Vinter, it became evident that the intention was that Spurgeon himself was to be the young preacher!

The subsequent remarks of Spurgeon about this Mr Vinter are very helpful to us here. He apparently was the most outstanding of the village preachers around Cambridge at the time. Spurgeon says:

> *His genial soul, warm heart, and kindly manner were enough to keep a whole fraternity stocked with love; and, accordingly, a goodly company of zealous workers belonged to the Association, and laboured as true yoke-fellows. My suspicion is, that he not only preached himself, and helped his brethren, but that he was a sort of recruiting sergeant, and drew in young men to keep up the number of the host.*[2]

It's not in the least surprising to me that such a loving and zealous man as Mr Vinter was surrounded by the young men of the church, because that man was a disciple-maker, and real disciple-makers attract disciples, no doubt because they love them!

Mr Vinter's method that day was a fairly rough way of training a very young believer. It's rather like throwing one's child into the water to get him to swim! I don't suggest it be copied. I certainly don't think it would have worked with me. I can still remember a time during my early years in India when I was put on the spot to speak; I had been given no preparative advice, and did not do at all well that night in the darkened village! I could hardly think of what to say to all those people. They were not only uneducated and spoke no English, but lived in desperately poor circumstances, and knew nothing at all of my God. Meanwhile, I knew nothing about them. It still makes me embarrassed when I remember that occasion.

But what we learn here is that in England in the 19th century there were leaders in the Church who gave beginners opportunities in Christian ministry. Spurgeon, by the way, was not an entirely unknown quantity at the time. His gifts were already evident as a youth, before he preached that first time. And Mr Vinter had noticed him.

So, if a man or woman in your church evidences abilities in leading people to Christ in a loving and attentive way, be alert to it and give them further opportunities and encouragement. The Church should see herself as a parent to the earnest disciple. And of course, concern for a child's education and development will be uppermost in a good parent's heart.

Giving such a person an opportunity to preach is, of course, not the only way to help him or her develop. More often than not, opportunities arise apart from those of preaching. So, when you find a promising person who has something of the loving heart of Christ for His people, and especially for those who are yet to believe, you could perhaps get that person to read the Scriptures in a meeting, speak briefly at the Lord's Supper, lead others in prayer, or perhaps even encourage them to invite some new believers around for a meal and a discussion of biblical truths. And as for those already being considered by the church for ministry, urge them to set time aside every week for personal evangelism in the square, or in the university, or over lunch after church, or urge them to set aside time for the personal and consistent care of some new or struggling believer. And, after all the above, talk with them about their endeavours!

As Loved Apprentices in the Church

Correct and teach them

When we look at the ministry of Jesus among His twelve men, we see how often He rebuked them. Their reactions to pressing or difficult circumstances and their responses to His words (or the words of other disciples) gave Him ample opportunity for comment. Jesus took up these opportunities for rebuke, not because He was exasperated with them, but because He is the Word who teaches a believer truth and who, as their Master, has the right to discipline. To discipline is, in part, to disciple.

Jesus came into the world not to condemn the world but to save it. That being true, His whole approach to training these twelve men was driven by this desire to save them from the sinful nature that lay behind their pride, their impatience and their blindness to truth. And, in saving them, to make them as He is – a servant, a lover of souls, and a fisher of men.

Just to give you a few examples of how naturally these occasions of rebuke occur in the Gospel accounts, look at Luke 22. It's a chapter full of rebukes and warnings to His disciples in the final hours of His life before the cross. It's a backdrop to the cross. It's a remarkable closing chapter to His training of the Twelve. Right in the middle of the Last Supper, a dispute takes place among the disciples. Jesus immediately comments on it. He gets to what is at the heart of their irritability and conceit, and speaks to their pride and longing to be at the top. Immediately following comes His comment to Peter, whom He warns in particular. But at the same time He also encourages Peter to listen to Him, and to resist the temptation when it came, assuring him of His prayer for him and of his ultimate restoration. Pride, however, was not to be silenced by His Master's warning. After boasting of his intended commitment, Peter is warned yet again by the Master.

This personal warning to Peter is then followed by what happened on the Mount of Olives, with Jesus warning all of His disciples of bitter things to come. They all must watch and pray. His warnings continue, this time in His brief but telling words to Judas, who was about to betray Him. Finally, there is a postscript to those warnings towards the end of the chapter, when the Master '...*turned and looked at Peter*' (Luke 22:61), a visual rebuke that broke the latter's heart, and a proof that all His warnings had been warranted.

Rebuke is what much of discipling is about. In fact, Christlike training is not possible without rebuke, since love disciplines the one who is loved (Hebrews 12:6). A brother rebukes a brother because he is a loving brother. '*If your brother sins, rebuke him, and if he repents, forgive him*' (Luke 17:3).

One of the leading reasons for believers being called into fellowships is so that they might be corrected and rebuked *within* the dynamic of a loving group of fellow believers. People do not generally grow well in Christ when they are outside the robust growing-conditions where the Gospel is preached and the Word taught and applied. Plants grown in glasshouses do not stand up well to the weather conditions of the open garden. The Church is like an open garden – dug over, planted and watered, vigorously weeded, and subject to all weather conditions.

We have the same difficulties today, in bringing loving rebuke to bear in the lives of fellow disciples, that I imagine Christians have had throughout the centuries. The fellowship of which James speaks in his short letter gives us an insight into how things should be within the Church. I especially love James 5:13-16, which speaks of true brotherhood and sisterhood that is open, transparent fellowship. These verses speak of spiritual conditions practised within the Church back then that are conducive to real growth in grace and the knowledge of Jesus.

Sadly, the picture these verses portrays seems a far cry from what the Church is like today, when most church attendees barely know who is sitting next to them! The spiritual and moral immaturity of so much present Christian living can probably be traced back to this superficiality of fellowship with one another. Such fellowship certainly does not allow for the discipline of mutual enquiry, comment, rebuke and correction.

Nothing but love for one another should drive these warnings and censures in the Church. I can remember the exact times and places I've been hurt by critical words, given in the main because of my immaturity. I hate pain and humiliation. My experience as a pastor through the course of fifty years in the ministry has left me with some painful memories of tellings-off at the hands of other church members. It seemed so often to be done in a public space, where lessons are most sharply felt, and humiliation is the deepest.

No one, myself included, likes to hear the truth about one's sinful behaviour or speech, nor likes others to hear those truths! There is no doubt that lessons at such moments will not be forgotten.

Painful rebuke operates like a camera taking informative shots. It captures and holds, in colour, the moment of the words of rebuke and the scene of the pain, and puts its pictures in an album for our memory to pick up and consider.

Hopefully I've learned something from those painful times, although real learning and change is not always the outcome. Too often it results in bitterness. It's my belief that when love's kindness and compassion accompany a rebuke, the lesson is even more etched into the memory and even more biting to the conscience – because love speaks the truth, and truth spoken in love especially hurts, just as the tears of parents over their son's foolishness leave marks on his conscience and memory that can never be erased. Christ's *look* at Peter, recorded in Luke 22:61, would never be forgotten by that disciple, nor will the Church ever forget!

Although appointed to leadership in the Church and gifted, the person who does the rebuking and the correcting is, of course, not the primary critic but rather the messenger of rebuke. The rebuke itself is in the Lord's Word, that is '...*living and active, sharper than any two-edged sword, piercing to the division of soul and of spirit, of joints and of marrow, and discerning the thoughts and intentions of the heart*' (Hebrews 4:12). It's the sword of the Spirit, which is the Word of God, that does the piercing – not the messenger. I say this because the messenger can very often usurp the Spirit's role and overstep the mark in bringing what he or she thinks is a correct and penetrating application of the Word to the brother or sister.

Our applications are where most of our exegesis of the Word of Christ goes wrong. Caution is needed in making such applications. The better the understanding of the text of the Bible, the more likely the application will be sound. One should essentially let the Scriptures do the rebuking. When the messenger of the rebuke is motivated by love and a longing for the well-being of his fellow believer, the Word will be carried to the heart with even greater force, because it is unimpeded by the discolouration of prejudice and emotion, and impelled by love.

When the messenger's words of rebuke are constrained and shaped by the Word itself, they carry real power. When the messenger of rebuke uses words that have no Word of Christ within them, there will likely be mere heat, force and unhappiness. Peter's preaching in Acts 2 is a good example of how rebuke is to be exercised. He quotes the prophetic Word of God, draws his conclusion about Jesus from the biblical text, and then finishes with a clear accusation which is entirely justified. And his hearers respond with urgent but welcome cries from their hearts for forgiveness.

The undeniable and indisputable importance of the place of the messenger of rebuke is evident in a passage such as Colossians 1:28-29: '*Him we proclaim, warning everyone and teaching everyone with all wisdom, that we may present everyone mature in Christ. For this I toil, struggling with all his energy that he powerfully works within me.'* And in James 5:19,20: *'My brothers, if anyone among you wanders from the truth and someone brings him back, let him know that whoever brings back a sinner from his wandering will save his soul from death and will cover a multitude of sins.'*

The one doing the rebuking always needs to remember the parable of the unmerciful servant in Matthew 18. When the one doing the rebuking feels a 'beam' to be more in his own eye than in the eye of the one being rebuked, then the words of rebuke and correction can only have a sweetness about them that wins the disciple over to making life changes for Jesus' sake!

Rebukes that are accepted can make all the difference between either our being crippled by a behaviour that is impure, or our establishing a new pattern of behaviour that frees us for years to come.

In the 19th century, rabbits and weasels from Britain, together with possums from Australia, were introduced into New Zealand, probably with the best of intentions. They were allowed to proliferate unchallenged for years, so that today they have become a major ecological disaster for the country. Millions of dollars are spent annually on their control and eradication. A disciple will understand how instructive this illustration is. Better to suffer rebuke and pain now, than one day to face the fact that a behaviour or belief has been allowed to become so entrenched as to be near unassailable and, sadly, synonymous with people's view of one's life and character.

Love them individually

One day, as I listened to Radio New Zealand, I heard a remarkable Afghani woman speaking of people in her country 'thirsting for love'. That remark holds true anywhere in the world, wherever men and women are to be found. It also holds true in the Church, especially in regards to disciple-making. Disciples are thirsting for the love of fellow disciples.

Just look at the Master with His twelve men, and see how loving a disciple-maker can be. The Scriptures are of course *full* of examples of His love! And why wouldn't they be, if we remember that He, being God, *is* love?

One of the most beautiful examples of this is found in Luke 22. His disciples had been arguing about who was the greatest. How could they have done such a thing, just as the Lord was leading them in that Last Supper? Easily, because as Paul the Apostle says, they were 'under sin', like all humankind. But what does Jesus say to these insensitive men? *'You are those who have stayed with me in my trials, and I assign to you, as my Father assigned to me, a kingdom'* (Luke 22:28,29). And, a few verses later on: *'Simon, Simon, behold, Satan demanded to have you, that he might sift you like wheat, but I have prayed for you that your faith may not fail. And when you have turned again, strengthen your brothers'* (Luke 22:31,32).

Here we see both the patience of love and the kindness of love in Jesus' training of these men. If this love of God the Father and of His Son for His own, for the Twelve, for Jerusalem, and for the lost is at the heart of the four accounts of the Gospel, then how can any aspect of Church life today (disciple-making included) begin to be of influence where the love of God is not present in the lives and practices of his people?

Love is closely associated with trust and trustworthiness. Love is 'faithful' (Galatians 5:22). The new young disciple will more often than not be a person with little or no real knowledge of the words and ways of Christ. He may come from a country that has virtually no Christian testimony, so that he hardly knows what a 'Christian' is. He may have no experience of assessing those who purportedly speak the truth.

Recently I met up with two new friends, both of whom know

very little of Christ, but who have placed their trust in me to lead them. They are immigrants to our country and, perhaps by virtue of that, more ready than others to trust in one who is older. It's an alarming trust, in a way. I want to get it right. I want them to love me. I don't want to let them down or in any way mislead them. I know I need to be absolutely trustworthy. I need to be doing it all entirely for Jesus, and not for some reason of my own. I need to be true to His Word.

I have been out evangelising in the public square in a suburban centre of our city, where we are planting a church. I'm not the only one out there. Other individuals who do not understand the Christian faith as I do are out there too, making a deliberate push for immigrants, whom they perceive to be more vulnerable and open to offers of help. The other day an immigrant friend of mine showed me a leaflet handed to him by one such person. He trusted me to put in the bin whatever I didn't agree with. The disciple-maker has a daunting responsibility. He represents Jesus' faithfulness to the truth and, in particular, His loving, faithful care of those who trust in Him.

The disciple-maker must give proof to these trusting friends who are sometimes just beginning their journey on the narrow way. He needs to prove that he is a trustworthy friend, with a love that is genuine and a commitment to their welfare and development that is transparent. Our lives need to be as open as our Christian testimonies. Right now in our church there are new immigrants who are at the door of Gospel life. What an enormous responsibility we have to lead them to Jesus and His words. When a friend asks to see Jesus, we must be ready to take him or her to that exact same Jesus whom those Greeks in John 12:20-22 asked to see, and to whom they were subsequently introduced. Nothing less will do.

Jesus was, of course, and still is, utterly trustworthy. The early disciples trusted in Him. They acknowledged that He and He alone could be trusted. When Jesus questioned them regarding their continuing trust in the face of others deserting Him, they said: *'Lord, to whom shall we go? You have the words of eternal life'* (John 6:68). Jesus was constantly seeking their trust. And they found Him entirely trustworthy as they put their trust in Him throughout the course of their lives. Jesus did not let them down. A disciple-maker is to emulate Christ in this regard. He or she should want very much to be reckoned as trustworthy by those who are being discipled.

A disciple-maker's trustworthiness is to be understood in this sense alone: that he or she leads people to Christ and His words.

Chapter 7

The Disciple-Maker's Goals for the Disciple

Some months ago I read a fantastic novel by Irving Stone entitled *The Agony and the Ecstasy*. It's about the great Renaissance artist Michelangelo. Something struck me forcibly – I had never realised just how staggeringly amazing the art and ability of a great sculptor are. I had never realised that such an artist can 'see' the finished form before he begins, and that very often he has no room for error, especially when his block of marble only allows him just enough space to execute his idea and no more.

When we take on the work of disciple-making, we need to 'see' Christian discipleship before we begin discipling the new believer. Mercifully, we don't have quite the same unforgiving constraints on us that the great Italian Renaissance artist had. However, we should 'see' a Christian disciple in the rough form that is presented to us in the person of the new believer. This person, who has just been rescued from a slavery of sorts in a dark kingdom, is the very person we are now to care for and help become a disciple of Christ.

But what are we to work towards? What are the goals for this new believer? For starters, we must be as sure as we can be that the one we are seeking to help is indeed a believer, that is, 'in Christ'. Nothing will come of trying to help a person grow as a Christian if that person is not 'in Christ'. I think it was my friend LeRoy Eims of The Navigators who told me about the dead stick and the living cutting analogy. If I plant a dead stick in the earth, then no end of watering and fertilising will make it grow. On the other hand, if I plant a living cutting (say of a rose or of hornbeam) and water that cutting and care for it, then I can expect it will strike, and a living plant will develop and eventually mature.

If I am to invest time as a disciple-maker in a person, any person, then I should have some confidence, some basis for believing, that that person is 'in Christ'. And the clearest marks of one being in Christ are that he or she will want to pray in Jesus' name and will want the 'milk of the word' – the Christian Scriptures and believe they are God's words.

What is the disciple-maker wanting to see happen in the life of this person who he or she has perhaps brought to Christ and who is now confessing their faith in Christ?

The disciple will confess the Lord Jesus Christ in the world

Jesus says in Matthew's Gospel that in making disciples, the Church needs to first baptise them *'in the name of the Father and of the Son and of the Holy Spirit'* (Matthew 28:19). What can we say of this command that is such an essential component of disciple-making? It is the inaugural action of faith of the new disciple in the Church and in the world.

It is no surprise therefore that in the Book of Acts baptism is what a newly-believing person submitted to at the very outset of his new life in Christ. Look at Acts 2:41: *'So those who received his word were baptised, and there were added that day about three thousand souls.'* Again, when looking for immediate and primary action following belief, consider Acts 8:36,38: *'And as they were going along the road they came to some water, and the eunuch said, "See, here is water! What prevents me from being baptised?" And he commanded the chariot to stop, and they both went down into the water... and he baptised him.'* In Acts 10:47,48 Peter is speaking of those people of

Cornelius' household who had just come to believe in Christ: '"*Can anyone withhold water for baptising these people, who have received the Holy Spirit just as we have?" And he commanded them to be baptised in the name of Jesus Christ.*' Other examples follow in this wonderful book, for example, Lydia's baptism: '*...The Lord opened her heart to pay attention to what was said by Paul. And after she was baptised, and her household as well, she urged us, saying, "If you have judged me to be faithful to the Lord, come to my house and stay"*' (Acts 16:14,15).

Then there is the jailer's baptism: '*And they spoke the word of the Lord to him and to all who were in his house... and he was baptised at once, he and all his family.*' (Acts 16:32,33). In each case the people being baptised had only just put their trust in the Lord. And in every case personal confession of faith in Jesus was the precursor of their baptism.

Nowadays we might be perturbed at this immediacy, and be hesitant to baptise before the candidate has passed some test of our making. But what are the simple, biblical tests for the new believer – does he or she have a desire to pray and a desire to hear His voice? Does he or she believe in His name for the forgiveness of sins?

Clearly baptism is not an unimportant thing in the life of Christian discipleship! It is the believer entering through the 'narrow gate' into a lifetime of obeying Christ's commands within whatever context she or he lives. It is the first act of obedience to which evangelism leads after people hear and believe.

As an act of obedience to Him who saves us from our sins, baptism is usually the disciple's first public confession (before the Church and the watching world) of his or her faith in the Lord Jesus. It's the biblical way of 'coming out', of 'coming up to the front'. It is when the believer announces the beginning of a new life and the end of the old. It is the believer's confession of having passed over from death to life through faith in Jesus. It is the new believer's identification with Him in His death. It is the lifting up of Christ's cross that the disciple must carry for the duration of his or her life, announcing to the world his or her faith in Christ's atoning death. It's the believer's initial step in joining with the Lord Jesus in His sufferings, *'...becoming like him in his death'* (Philippians 3:10). It should be seen by all disciples to be a privilege when called on to carry that cross! The believer is now one with Christ in His sufferings. He or she joins Simon from Cyrene in a fellowship of the cross. On that fateful day, Simon carried Jesus' cross and, in having his name recorded in the Scriptures, was given lasting honour (Mark 15:21).

How deeply sad it should be that baptism has become, like the Lord's Supper, an expected nicety within the fellowship of the Church – not always taken seriously and sometimes, appallingly, considered optional! This is a far cry from how it is viewed by new believers in those places where the Gospel is hated and where to be baptised is potentially a dangerous act of faith. These believers face it sometimes with trepidation! With that in mind, how can we be indifferent towards this inaugural action of the Christian? How can we be indifferent to what Christ has commanded?

The disciple will love the Lord Jesus Christ

The Gospel is Christ. He is the whole of this good news announced in the Bible. And so Jesus, having begun His preaching with the words, *'Repent, for the kingdom of heaven is at hand'*, then says, *'Follow me'* (Matthew 4:17,19). He is the good news. This is why He appoints the Twelve *'...so that they might be with him...'* (Mark 3:14).

The words of the Great Commission establish the central importance of Jesus in the believer's life. His commands are to be taught and obeyed. His authority and His presence are affirmed as fundamental to the carrying out of His Great Commission. Christ is everything in the believer's salvation from sin and death, and nothing the believer is or does warrants or earns this salvation. Christ alone is our Saviour.[1]

Why would anyone want to be baptised in Jesus' name if she or he was not profoundly grateful to this Saviour? Why would anyone want to obey Christ's commands if they did not love him? A love for Christ is not something a human teacher can give a disciple. The unbelieving person doesn't have any natural love for Jesus. But that love is given to everyone the Lord draws to Himself. Anyone who belongs to Jesus will love Him and love His Word. These are the disciple's new irrepressible instincts. The Lord has put a new song in his or her heart – a song of love for Jesus.

As I write, along our rural street there are lambs being born in every paddock, and it is truly lovely to see their instinct for their mother's milk. After being born they are on their feet in thirty or so minutes, and they circle their mothers, seeking that colostrum, that first milk. It is wonderful, too, to see them find their own mothers, even when all is in confusion after the entry of the farmer's dog into their field. They can hear the voice of their mother in the midst of all the noise of the bleating flock. In the same way, a new believer knows Jesus' voice among all the voices in this world, and loves Jesus as Lord from the very outset of his or her new life in Christ. The believer's heart is one that knows the love of Christ.

This love for Jesus, whilst present in the heart of the saved person from the beginning of his or her new life, may be strengthened through asking the Lord for more and more of that love – so that the disciple might truly love the Lord God with all his or her heart and mind (Deuteronomy 6:5). This 'all' stretches the disciple's efforts to the maximum, and sets the bar of attainment at the highest point. Nothing less is appropriate for the Lord of Glory! There are evidently no limits to our knowing in our own experience the love of God in Christ, says Paul in Ephesians 3:18. This is a truly wonderful prospect for a new believer – to enjoy Christ with the hope of ever-opening discoveries of His beauty. No human relationship, however delightful, can match it in its ongoing revelations of a loveliness of warmth and understanding. Walking with Christ is a continual, deepening morning in spring that lasts a lifetime.

To love Jesus is to obey Jesus

Immediately following baptism in Matthew 28:19,20 is a reference to that same person's obedience. Christian discipleship is essentially about the pursuit of obedience to Christ. As I said at the outset of this chapter, there can be no hope of obedience unless a person is saved. He or she has to be one who has received the Word. And where Christ's Word is received, it is loved, and when it is loved, it will be obeyed, and when it is obeyed, the believer is loved by the Saviour. Obedience is the goal of our faith – it is faith's expression (Romans 1:5, 16:26). The disciple's obedience is the intended end of the Lord's eternal love for the believer. It will not be otherwise for any disciple of Christ (1 Peter 1:2). To understand this is to understand the goal of disciple-making.

Having established this point, only now may we go on to speak of the disciple-maker as the one who puts in the hours and the time to encourage and help the new believer to obey. With these words, '...*teaching them to observe all that I have commanded you...*' (Matthew 28:20), Jesus is acknowledging and commanding the presence of the Church in the learning process. It is within the Church that the teacher and the pupil are engaged over the years in the pursuit of obedience. But this pursuit does not always go smoothly.

Jesus was amazed by the slowness of his twelve disciples to understand Him. You can see something of His disappointment in His words: '*O foolish ones, and slow of heart to believe all that the prophets have spoken!*' (Luke 24:25), '*Where is your faith?*' (Luke 8:25), and '*Have I been with you so long, and you still do not know me, Philip?*' (John 14:9) If the Twelve were not able to learn their lessons with

Him as their teacher, is it any wonder that new believers, having their fellow believers as teachers, will fail and stagger along the way?

Still today, believers of long-standing continue to disappoint both themselves and their teachers. Learning to obey His commands goes against the grain of human nature because there is a law at work within us which is waging war against the law of our minds (Romans 7). It will never be easy to '*...take every thought captive to obey Christ*' (2 Corinthians 10:5). Our thoughts are slippery and elusively deceptive. No part of our body takes kindly to being offered in slavery to righteousness (Romans 6:16). That is a slavery and sacrifice that our sinful hearts rebel at. Our culture pushes against the Word of Christ; young people especially are at the mercy of its pressures to conform, but the old, the poor and the wealthy are not exempt!

If we as disciple-makers have our feet firmly in this world (as we should), we will find ourselves having to address all the difficult ethical questions that will inevitably be faced in this age of moral relativism and denial of objective absolutes. Issues such as abortion, marriage, gender and sexuality may be difficult to navigate and may prove to be confrontational and divisive; but they need to be addressed by the Christian disciple. Then there are issues of personal and moral failure, such as addiction, guilt and shame. These too are part of the Christian's life, and as such need to be considered. Also there are questions about the exclusivity of the Christian faith in an age of pluralism, and questions around the nature of the Bible. All of these ought to be faced in our pursuit of obedience.

So the teacher needs to be loving, gentle and patient with the believer, who is his or her fellow disciple. The disciple-maker needs the wisdom, insight and understanding that the Holy Spirit alone can give, if he or she is to be successful in encouraging obedience in the one learning Christ.

We mustn't underestimate the difficulty of this pursuit of obedience. Jesus' words in Matthew 28 leave us in no doubt that a life-long pursuit of obedience is what He envisaged. The struggle won't lessen anytime soon! The lesson is never done. As the gardener needs to provide a depth of soil for a plant to flourish, so the disciple-maker needs to plant the Word of God deeply – through thorough, continual and patient encouragement of the disciple, who in turn needs an open and wistful heart that welcomes the Saviour and His Word.

The disciple will love the fellowship of those in Christ

To me the most fascinating reference to Christian fellowship in the New Testament is that of 1 John 1:3. The word 'fellowship' is used here in regard to our companionship, community and sharing with one another as believers, and also in regard to our companionship with God the Father and God the Son. Entering into the latter, through faith in Jesus Christ, leads one into the former – with believers.

Our salvation from sin will always lead to such a fellowship with others, for there is no such creature, in the Scriptures' estimation of a Christian, who can remain outside the fellowship of believers whilst still being within the fellowship of the Father, Son and Holy Spirit. We are saved by the Lord into fellowship with other believers. The fellowship with the Father and the Son is that of believers who together trust in the Lord, and who together wholly rely on Him as people He has bought with His own blood.

John's short letter is primarily evangelistic. He is writing so that people might believe in Jesus whom he, John, has seen and confesses as Lord. His second purpose seems no less wonderful – that his readers might join him in fellowship with one another. This fellowship on earth was a very lovely thing to John, so much so that he longed to share this fellowship with his readers by urging them to also believe on the Lord Jesus.

The very earliest Christians were 'devoted' to fellowship with one another (Acts 2:42). Paul's letters prove, amongst other things, that people must have seen very dramatic changes in these new believers in Christ – they had begun to love people who previously had been strangers to them, even people who would have been of a very different race and social standing. Slaves now sat with masters, and people who had previously been idolaters, adulterers, homosexuals, thieves, drunkards and slanderers were now found sitting alongside everyone else – transformed, and very different people to what they had once been (1 Corinthians 6:11). They were now morally transformed people who loved one another! Their fellowship with one another must have been the wonder of the age! Such fellowship still should be!

As Christians under the New Testament, we are hardly ever commanded to meet with one another, but we are very frequently told to love one another. This is because meeting together will never be an issue when we love one another. Love wants to gather up others into its arms. So the disciple-maker is to teach the disciple – not about church-going or regular attendance at meetings, but rather that he or she must love other brothers and sisters as Jesus has loved us and given His life for us. Jesus crossed oceans that separated worlds, as it were, so as to come from His glory of joy into our dark and miserable backyard, in order to bring us to His joy. His love didn't look over the fence at our sorrow and brokenness; it rather piled into our homes with food for the table of our hearts. Christian fellowship is His love for us, received and then shared with and among His people.

Importantly, it's in this fellowship of brothers and sisters that we confess Him and learn to obey His commands. It's in this fellowship of love that we are rebuked and corrected, and take lessons to heart. It's here in this fellowship that we confess our sins and pray for one another, cry with one another, share the Lord's

Discipling Like the Master

Supper in deep thankfulness for Jesus' love for us, give our offerings out of joyful hearts, listen to the Gospel being preached, study how to apply His Word in our world, and ultimately together seek Him. Christian fellowship is His classroom for our learning hearts.

CHAPTER 8

Examples of Disciple-Making

My Christian life was never going to be the same once I met my American friend LeRoy Eims in 1976. Like young men and women everywhere, I desperately wanted a mentor – and he became just that for me. He totally won my heart over to discipling like the Master. I only wish that, in the years that followed, I had not at times let the demands of leading a congregation shake my youthful vision. A full-time Christian ministry is never easy to do well. It's so common to take too much notice of others' successes, and to be persuaded that numerical growth is a measure of the quality of one's ministry. How easy it is to be frequently distracted from one's principal goals by criticism and unhappiness within the Church. All of this can muddy the waters so that the designated path becomes overgrown with weeds and unclear.

Every believer is unique
In this chapter I'll give you some examples and make some general observations concerning my more recent discipling. I hope this will encourage you to think more deeply about this ministry in regard to yourself and your church. Each of these examples of disciple-making is, as it should be, very different – because, like the trees of the forest, each person is an individual and has his or her own 'voice' and 'features'.[1]

A new disciple comes into the disciple-maker's life at a particular time in his or her life, and with unique needs – spiritually, morally and in relation to his or her giftedness within the Church. Consequently there is no exact template for the disciple-maker to follow. So the idea of going on some course for six weeks and adopting a one-size-fits-all approach to this ministry should be dismissed out of hand as both suspect and unworthy of a brother or sister's individuality – just as the raising of a child is not done well when parents or schools follow a rigid pattern. There needs to be some room in the home that allows for individual expression and development; otherwise that child will not have the quiet confidence that goes with being respected as a unique person in Christ.

This afternoon my wife has been sitting out in the sunshine under our veranda, knitting a jumper for a grandson. She's following the instructions of a pattern, and I've already seen her at least once unpick work because something was not done as it should have been. Thankfully disciple-making is not pursued along the same lines. The Holy Spirit doesn't follow some set programme when training a person. He's artistic; He is always original. No one is taught in the same way as another. However, in every case the lesson is the same – Christ.

The general focus of our meetings together

Individuality aside, there can be said to be a general plan that, when followed, gives shape to discipling. What is this plan? And what common factors will be found in this training?

First of all, the Lord Jesus is to be central to the meeting. He's the subject of our discussion, the recipient of our love and the acknowledged Giver of our every spiritual longing. His words are of necessity to be the centre of our mind's attention and our heart's love. First and foremost, we read His Word, the Scriptures, studying them and meditating on them together. Prayer (which is

Examples of Disciple-Making

faith's voice) necessarily follows, since the Lord has spoken to us and now looks forward to the outpouring of the meditation of our hearts – our expressions of deepest gratitude, our confession of sin, and our assertions of trust and hope in Him. And then, together in Christ and remaining in his Word, we talk with each other about our Lord and Saviour (Malachi 3:16). These are the essential ingredients needed for disciple-making. They are the big-brush strokes (in various colours) on the canvas of our times together in Christ, and they give those times balance, depth and perspective.

I can clearly recall my excitement when, as a young believer and pastor, a list of Bible verses was given to me. I was taught how to memorise these verses and, more importantly, what the benefits of memorising the Bible were to the believer. I took all this on board eagerly and relished every minute of memorising those 60 verses that year. I still love sharing with new believers diagrams like the Word Hand, with its five fingers (beginning with the smallest) representing hearing, reading, studying, memorising and meditating on the Word, and explaining how the Word is truly able to be gripped by the mind and heart when all five 'fingers' (especially the 'thumb', representing meditation) are used by the believer. Such simple things were delightful to me as a young learner of Christ.

But don't misunderstand me! Discipling is not about a believer passing a list of achievement levels that an examiner can check off as done. That approach would reduce discipling to a narrow and finite programme, when it isn't. It's a good work that's begun with faith in Jesus as Lord and has its conclusion in eternity (Philippians 1:6).

All times spent together as believers should have as their focus Christ and His words, and at all moments we should strive to maintain that focus. It may be that you are reading a particular biography or looking at some piece of theology together. It may be that you have read Psalm 42:1 together and are now confessing to having too little of that same longing for a knowledge of God as the Psalmist had. It may be that you are discussing the brief talk that you, as a younger believer, gave at the Lord's Supper in church the previous Sunday morning. Or maybe you are confessing to being ashamed of a word you used in a conversation with another believer after church. Whatever the reason for these times together as brothers and sisters in Christ, a true disciple-maker will endeavour to ensure that everything is directed toward learning Christ and observing all that He has taught.

Illustrations of disciple-making

In the following examples, precise biographical detail and actual names have been avoided (and even the capital letters that have been substituted have no relation to real names).

Also, I want to make it clear that my part in the discipling of these men is just that – a *part* (and often a brief part, at that) among the many parts and contributions of God's people toward the development of the individual believer in Christ. A disciple-maker who thinks otherwise has forgotten his or her place, which is as a member among many members within the Body of Christ, His Church.

P came into my life from another church. I liked him because he was willing to address his lack of self-control and confess his general spiritual weakness as a professing Christian. We met on a number of occasions to address these matters, and to look at how to overcome sin. But his real issue centred around whether or not he was in Christ. His need to be quite clear with himself as to whether or not he was in Christ was discussed on nearly every occasion of our being together. And, of course, that was as it should have been, because there is no more important question facing a human being than this. What proof was there of his being in Christ? An open ownership of one's sin is a primary mark of true faith in Christ. Was that evident? Was there in him an ownership that his sin was an offence principally against the Lord's rule, and something that grieves Him? *'Against you, you only, have I sinned and done what is evil in your sight...'* (Psalm 51:4). The New Testament quotes the prodigal son as saying: *'Father, I have sinned against heaven and before you...'* (Luke 15:21).

Openness of heart about one's sinfulness before man and God is the beginning of wisdom, and little progress can be made in discipleship without it. I particularly appreciated his openness to me. One may be frank and open with a friend. In the end, those times together petered out. However, they were not wasted. Of late, he's come back into my life. That can only be a sign of better things to come, I think! And here's a question – why did he come back into my life? Almost certainly because he believes I care for him. What were the ingredients of those times together? Every one of them was different, but there was always the Bible, always prayer, always frank discussion and the challenge to be true to one's confession of faith, and always an emphasis on 'a broken and contrite heart' as the prerequisite of experiential union with Christ, and the basis of enjoying the assurance of His love.

Q came into my life as a new Christian. His way of life until his conversion may have been condoned by society generally, but not by the Lord Jesus. By the grace of God he had felt convicted, and he was led to repent and to believe the Gospel. He now wanted true friendship, brotherhood and, most especially, ongoing conversation with a Christian brother about his previous way of life in the light of the Scriptures. Such discussions can only be pursued by two people who together realise their respective, profound and ongoing need of a Saviour. That is to say, the disciple-maker and the disciple are and always ought to be brothers or sisters who together know themselves to be under His grace. Such discussions may have no end, because sin's previous night may have been so prolonged that its presence may remain on the edges of the soul as a lingering border of some shadow-land. Yet we thanked the Lord for these shadows, and we were grateful for even the deepest ones – for they bring a depth and perspective to our lives that those who have gone through life morally unscathed by more troubling sins may not have.[2]

D came into the Church with a deeply religious background. He knew only a 'form' of Christianity, not Christ himself. And then, wonderfully, he was brought to Christ through the love and persuasive arguments of a member of his family. I began meeting with him as a new believer. These meetings generally began with his asking some question pertaining to his life or ministry in the church. Discussion of the Bible and life, prayer and coffee were their ingredients. He appeared to love these times together, and that's a very good thing, for it's a long road to eternal life, and few travel it. And to travel it alone is not what anyone would want.

Good company on this long and difficult journey is so heartwarming! Fellowship with a brother or sister is a privilege that not all pilgrims have. They walk by themselves, with no one to cheer them along when things are hard and discouraging. So when such company is found, don't let it go! I've come to see that unless a new believer particularly wishes for your company, and is hungry to learn Christ from you and alongside you, there is little likelihood of your travelling together. So what kind of company should a new believer seek? Loving company! People generally do not ask for help in churches in which they see little evidence of love. This fact should challenge us, because it reminds the Church that teaching or knowing the Gospel is not enough. Along with truth, one needs to be given a heart that loves and is prepared to give to others at a cost to self. The Gospel is an infinitely precious gift to give, and as such it is best given wrapped up in a heart full of thoughtful and sincere love (1 Thessalonians 2:8).

I knew T when he was a boy, but when he became a young man he ceased growing in Christ because he hadn't grown enough in the knowledge of His Word. I guess he came back to me because he trusted me and wanted to find some Christian anchor, a mentor that would lead him back to that old path which he had left. Those meals we had together were so good, but the times of confession of need and prayer for one another were better by far! Afterwards I remembered him in my prayers almost every day. How can a disciple-maker ever forget a human being as ready to own his need of Christ as T was? To be successful in disciple-making one needs to be faithful in prayer.

It doesn't happen often, but sometimes in life, people follow you to your next assignment, to be with you and part of your work. E is this kind of man. I was so grateful that he joined our church-planting work. Only lately, when I realised his importance to the future church, did I move to invest heavily in his life and training. I now meet with him every week. With our giving to him greater responsibilities in the church there have come greater expectations; and, with that, greater openness in critiquing not only his public work but at times his character, and even on occasions his words. Sometimes nothing of great importance comes up in our weekly meetings – one can't eat steak at every meal! That's life and that's discipling; some days are ordinary, whilst others are wonderfully memorable.

I'm very aware of the wisdom of 2 Timothy 2:2, where Paul outlines an approach for Timothy to follow as a leader of the Church

Discipling Like the Master

– always keep in view the next runner in the relay race of Gospel ministry.

This reminds me of the Norfolk Island Kentia palms in our garden. If you look carefully, you will see that there within each new frond that unfolds is yet another one already being formed! That in itself is a parable of multiplication and the need for passing on the truth of the Gospel. Time is short. The day is fading. It is time well spent when one keeps contributing to the training of His people – while there still is the opportunity to do so.

The next man I want to tell you about is R, whom I met on a university campus. I first knew him only by sight, and we smiled when we passed each other. Then one day he approached me and told me that he had been watching me throughout the year, and that he wanted me to tell him about Jesus. How can a Christian turn away from an invitation like that? When I asked him at our first meeting together what he wanted to be, he told me that he wanted to be a righteous man. Now that is a tremendous starting point! He was, by his own admission, an abject failure in his quest for that righteousness. This man needed to look at Paul's letter to the Romans, and most of our times together that followed were spent doing just that.

For three years we met together, and when this period came to an end I was fairly confident that he understood that only through being 'in Christ' could one ever be righteous. Only then could he know the righteousness that is from God through faith. More importantly by far, I have every confidence that he is in that precious place. In the years since, I pray for him virtually every day. I'm praying that when I next see him my confidence in his having confessed Jesus as his righteousness will ultimately prove to have been well placed. A disciple-maker prays for those he gives his life to.

Examples of Disciple-Making

I feel I could not omit one final example of disciple-making from this account, because it took place over a number of decades, and in a different culture to my own, namely India. Over a period of twenty-five years I have spent several weeks per year in intense interaction with many young Indian men. Those weeks in Pune, and in the beautiful hills of the Nilgiris in southern India, together formed a kind of long, intermittent, rambling conversation. Those times were something like a Christian ashram that was reconvened year by year. It was life together to a wonderful level – brief, intense and demanding. The overall goal was to foster an understanding of the Gospel, and to learn to live within its truth within both the Church and the world. I went to India over those twenty-five years to invest in the lives of these men, who for the most part were preparing for the ministry of the Gospel or were already actively involved in it. Many, but not all, returned year by year. I went there as a disciple-maker, in the hope of making some real theological impression on their understanding of the Gospel, and with the hope that, like some dripping tap on a stone bench, my ministry would leave through the years an indelible mark on their characters and lives.

I'm writing this book in large part for the sake of those many young friends in India and Sri Lanka, because I want them to be able to have something to remember me and my ministry by. I want them to have a record of what I believe, and why I loved them so much and came back each year. Those were some of the happiest times in my life, there amidst the tea plantations of the beautiful Nilgiris and under the mango trees in the intense heat of Pune, Maharashtra. I have wonderful memories of us reading together great books such as *Authority* by M.L. Jones, *God's Words* by J.I. Packer, *The Great Exchange* by J. Bridges and B. Bevington, *The Unfolding Mystery* by E.P. Clowney and *A Vision for Missions* by T. Wells.

I hope these few very brief sketches have been of interest to you in relation to discipling. These people never belonged to me. They never were mine, even when it was through me that they believed. The Lord brings them to us for a time, and a disciple-maker gives them what he can give of the Gospel and himself. Every meeting together matters. Not every meeting will be momentous, but every meeting ought to be in Christ. Make Jesus, crucified and living, and His words central to every such meeting. Sometimes those times together were few in number, and sometimes they continued for years. Sometimes little progress was made, and at other times I was able to look back and be amazed at change for the better. But every one was a privilege I looked forward to. Today, I continue to meet with certain men in the church on a regular basis. My public ministry is lessening. But the ministry of the Word can go on through the years in a more personal way.

CLOSING CADENZA

A Meditation on Themes of Disciple-Making

'Those who sow in tears shall reap with shouts of joy!' (Psalm 126:5)

I was brought up in a region of New Zealand called the Waikato. My father was a dairy farmer and a lover of gardening. As a child it seemed to me that we had enormous vegetable gardens, and I remember long, long rows of potatoes and sweet potatoes (called kumara). We would plant the seed potatoes and kumara in the beautiful volcanic black earth. I remember hoeing and mounding the earth over those kumara as they grew, and then much later, when the plants had died back under summer's heat, I would enjoy the wonder and be amazed by the discovery of hidden surprises. The uncovering of new potatoes, in my child's heart, ranked in scale of wonders right up alongside finding newly-hatched ducklings under the hissing Muscovy duck (who nested in the hollow of the walnut tree beside the dog kennel). In Dad's garden we would uncover what seemed to me to be a multiplicity of wonderfully-fresh potatoes, their skins translucent over the white flesh, the damp, dark earth still clinging to them. And there, in the middle of this uncovered mystery, was an even greater mystery – the rotting seed potato that had begun it all. That single potato was now nothing. It had once been everything. It now was left in the ground to rot. It had done its job. It had given its life.

Jesus observed this very same phenomenon – not of course with the South American potato, but with wheat and barley seeds. And, wonderful, timeless preacher that He was, He used it to illustrate the cost of discipleship in the service of the Master. And, more importantly, the cost to God the Father, who '...*gave his only Son...*' (John 3:16), and the cost to the Son, who '...*gave himself for me*' (Galatians 2:20).

The Irish potato famine took place from 1845 to about 1851, at a time when about two-thirds of the population of Ireland was dangerously dependent on one or two varieties of potato. When those varieties got blight and their crops began to seriously fail, a million or so people died, and another one to two million fled to Canada, the United States and Australia. The famine devastated Ireland.

I've often thought how dreadfully fearful and anxious those people must have been throughout those years. They went out to plant their precious seed potatoes, all the time knowing that their families needed those very same potatoes that very day for a meal, and yet knowing too that the planting of such precious seed was their only hope of their making it through the coming winter. Those starving families had to plant the very food they needed that day, if they were to eat any food at all in the year to come.

This pain of loss in giving, and the fear and anxiety in the sowing of precious seed, is evidenced in Psalm 126. But so too is the promise of the joy of the harvest that would follow. *'Those who sow in tears shall reap with shouts of joy! He who goes out weeping, bearing the seed for sowing, shall come home with shouts of joy, bringing his sheaves with him'* (Psalm 126:5,6). The loss of the seed was the necessary precursor to the multiplication of that seed, and the farmer's tears were the forerunner to the family's subsequent joy.

This same principle of 'loss for gain' which Jesus taught in John 12:24-26 was applied by Paul in 1 Corinthians 15 to Jesus' death and resurrection, and to the death and resurrection of our bodies.

There first needs to be the death and burial of our bodies, before there can ever be the hope of the resurrected and glorified body. Most importantly, there had to be the death and burial of Christ's body, before there could ever be His resurrection – the '*...first-fruits...*' (1 Corinthians 15:23) of the subsequent harvest of resurrected bodies on that last and great day. *'What you sow does not come to life unless it dies'* (1 Corinthians 15:36). Paul had Jesus to thank for this principle which he so powerfully applied to our lives.

In John 12 this principle of *death before life*, of *loss before gain*, of *loss for gain*, is applied by Jesus in two ways. It is firstly applied to the death and resurrection of the Master Himself. He had spoken of His death in verse 7, and then again, most significantly in these words: *'The hour has come for the Son of Man to be glorified'* (John 12:23). In the previous chapter, His great statement that He is *'...the resurrection and the life'* (John 11:25), presupposes His death while at the same time affirms His never-ending life. Jesus then takes up this principle of death before life as He continues in John 12:27, speaking of this in which He would glorify the Father's name. The Lord uses this particular word 'glory' to speak of all that was to be accomplished in His death and resurrection. The Father and the Son were to be 'glorified' in His death and resurrection. This word is filled with the ideas of magnificence, fulfilment, accomplishment and hope! Despite all appearances to the contrary, His death was His glorification; or rather, His death together with His burial, resurrection and exaltation was His glorification. His own people would be saved through His death. He would then be glorified in the presence of the Father, with the glory He had had before the world began (John 17:5).

When we think of the cross, we think not only of His enemies' determination to kill Him, but also of the Lord's will to put his Son to death (Isaiah 53:10, Acts 2:23, 4:28). But these factors alone are not enough to correctly understand the cross. Jesus Himself chose the cross. Read what powerful words John writes: *'Now is my soul troubled. And what shall I say? "Father, save me from this hour"? But for this purpose I have come to this hour. Father, glorify your name'* (John 12:27,28). His refusal to pursue any will other than the Father's, and His choosing the cross, is directly linked to the subsequent extraordinary accomplishment devolving from His death – which we see so powerfully expressed in John 12:32: *'And I, when I am lifted up from the earth, will draw all people to myself.'* Here we see a unique fruitfulness; a fruitfulness that no other person or prophet, however spiritual, could ever achieve. By His death and resurrection, He saved His people from their sins.

This principle of death before life is secondly applied to our lives as His disciples. Here our fruitfulness as believers is contingent upon our following the Master (John 12:26). And where did our Master go? If I had been there in Galilee and Judea with Jesus and had followed in His steps (1 Peter 2:21), where would they have taken me?

Before he gives us His answer to that question, Jesus first tells us that there are two ways of living in this world: *'Whoever loves his life loses it, and whoever hates his life in this world will keep it for eternal life'* (John 12:25). The first way of life mentioned bears no relation to Christ. The traveller on this road 'loves his life', and does not keep the Master's steps in view, but rather follows a course of life that bears no resemblance to Him. This is what we might call normal human living, where there is a rejection of the Lord's sovereignty over him as a human being and sinner, and an elevation of self over others and over the Master's will. The result is a 'bare cupboard' so to speak. In this way of life we see the prospect of a kind of famine. We see a potato on the shelf, seemingly as good as new, but alone – a 'single seed' in life and a 'single seed' at life's close; a fine specimen of a seed, but unused and unfruitful. We see nothing of the wonderful uncovering of those fresh white potatoes in the volcanic earth that I saw as a child. This is not life as Jesus wants it to be. It is the very opposite of Christ's life, for we see in the Lord Jesus Christ's submission to His Father's will at all times, even at the point of His deepest sorrow and agony on the cross.

But then there is a second, alternative way of life that Jesus refers to. Here the person wants to live as the Master was and continues to be, giving His life for His people. This disciple will 'hate his life' (John 12:25, Luke 14:26). This shocking expression that Jesus uses to describe a certain way of life is elaborated upon in Philippians 2, and epitomised in the following words: *'Do nothing from rivalry or conceit, but in humility count others more significant than yourselves...'* (Philippians 2:3). It is then immediately illustrated in the words that follow in Philippians 2:6-8, in a beautiful picture of the Son and His chosen humiliation, where He *'...made himself nothing...'* (Philippians 2:7).

This life of true Christian discipleship is further described in Mark 8:34: *'...If anyone would come after me, let him deny himself and take up his cross and follow me.'* Be careful here, for it would be unfortunate if we understood this second way of life simply in terms of self-denial. To do that would be to seriously misstate the Christian life. Christian discipleship is more than mere self-denial. 'Discipleship,' says Bonhoeffer, *'means allegiance to the suffering Christ.'*[1] That is to say, if we're to understand Christian discipleship correctly, the focus will be not exclusively on self-denial (expelling whatever draws one away from holiness) so much as on the Saviour Himself, and on His sufferings for us in particular. When we 'serve' this Christ and 'follow' this Christ, we will be fruitful in life (John 12:26).

How can we understand this fruitfulness? The rewards for our living this life of allegiance to Christ are the complete opposite of those awaiting the one who 'loves his life'. The one who serves the

Discipling Like the Master

Master and follows in His steps is the same one who is 'honoured' by the Father (John 12:26). In the context of the dying seed which brings forth many seeds, and of His call for us as believers to be as He is in his death and resurrection, surely we can assume that this 'honour' has something of that fruitfulness Jesus knows through his being 'lifted up'(John 12:32).

The fruitfulness spoken of in John 12:20-24 (and perhaps John 15:5 as well) is often understood as referring to further growth in grace; but might not it refer equally to our seeing people come to Christ through our life and ministry? After all, the context here is certain Greeks coming to Jesus, and multitudes of people being drawn to Him through His cross. And the principle in verse 24 of the single seed and the many seeds that follow that seed's death is clearly intended to apply to both Jesus and to His followers in a similar way. The disciple who 'dies' for Christ is the same disciple who is multiplied by discipling others. Others may come in repentance and faith to Christ through that person. Others may be deeply impressed by his or her life in Christ, and as a consequence come to love the Lord more.

Jesus' promise to believers who give their lives to the Saviour is remarkable. We are only a single seed. But so much can come of that single seed. Think of the biblical illustration of the 'boy' who had 'five barley loaves and two fish'. This story of the feeding of the five thousand (John 6:1-15) is found in all of the four Gospel accounts, because of its importance in establishing the identity of Christ. However, only in John's Gospel is the giver described as a 'boy'. Each of the four writers notes the very small number of loaves and fish. I like John's additional emphasis of 'boy' very much, because it underlines the limitations and the sheer impossibility, as far as the Twelve were concerned, of ever meeting the needs of so many. The apostles saw no prospect of such a little child's lunch being transformed into lunches for thousands. Their misplaced focus on the gulf between the little and the many to be fed sadly proves beyond any doubt that the Master's previous miracles, amazingly, had not left them confident in His ability to meet all challenges and overcome them. In stark contrast to their unbelief is the boy's self-sacrifice – unstated, but nonetheless clear.

The result of this small lunch being put into the hands of the Master was an explosion of plenty from very little. The thousands there that day ate *'as much as they wanted'* (John 6:11).

I remember in 2011 walking from our car along a path in a mountain village in Andalusia, Spain. We walked through a coloured carpet of persimmons, olives and chestnuts. I've never seen so much plenty and so much waste, such a profusion of fruit on the ground. The explanation for it all was that the villagers had abandoned their homes and gardens and had moved to the cities, so there was no one to harvest the plenty. This superabundance is what Jesus is talking about in John 12:23-26, when He speaks of the 'many seeds', and His 'honouring' the one who follows Him, and of His being 'glorified' through His death. So much has been given to the Son, and so much will be given to the believer who loses his life for Christ's sake and the Gospel. *'Truly, I say to you, there is no one who has left house or brothers or sisters or mother or father or children or lands, for my sake and for the gospel, who will not receive a hundredfold now in this time...'* (Mark 10:29-30).

William Burns was an highly effective preacher in Scotland before he left for China, where he worked for twenty years, eventually dying in near obscurity in 1868. In his ministry in China he proved to be equally extraordinary as a missionary as he had been a preacher in Scotland. In the first five years of his work in Swatow, just thirty-nine converts were received into the Church; yet by 1911 nearly four and a half thousand people had subsequently been baptised.[2] A little seed, sown in relative obscurity, had brought forth a great harvest in the years that followed.

Before Jesus spoke about the single seed producing the many seeds, certain Greeks had come asking to see Him (John 12:20-22). Their coming was evidently a matter of tremendous importance and significance to Jesus. His 'answer' to their coming was a burst of comments in John 12:23-26 on the worth of His death and of ours for Him.

I want you, the reader, to long for this fruitfulness that He promises to His disciples. The alternative to that life of fruitfulness in Christ is too terrible to think of – a life of barrenness as far as Christ is concerned, of emptiness like that of a mountain call without an echo, or a pantry during a famine, or a lonely soul in a crowded place – with few, if any, hearing of Jesus through us and, by His grace, coming to faith in Him. For the Christian, all that matters is what concerns Jesus; all that matters is what He thinks of our lives.

As that life-giving Seed that fell to the ground and died, Jesus is now surrounded by His people, whom He calls His 'brothers' and His 'children'. I sincerely hope that in reading this book, you will appreciate more than ever how completely confident we should be that this same Lord, upon whom we depend, will use us His children to bring others to Him (John 10:16).

Jesus truly is *'...the resurrection and the life'* (John 11:25). As we face His final command to make disciples in this world in which we live – a world that is seriously divided at many levels, and knows such raw inequalities, and is so full of fear about what tomorrow will bring – let us encourage one another as brothers and sisters to look to Jesus alone for the desire and strength to follow Him.

Notes

Introduction

1. J. Oswald Sanders, *Problems of Christian Discipleship*, OMF Books, first printed 1958, this edition 1974, p. 137.
2. For an excellent remark on the continuing work of Christ in the Church, see John Murray, *Collected Writings*, The Banner of Truth Trust, 1976, Vol.1. Chapter 19 'The Power of the Holy Spirit', p. 141.

Chapter 1. He Called Them to Be with Him

1. Dr & Mrs Howard Taylor, *Hudson Taylor and the China Inland Mission*, R&R Clark, 1949, p. 407.
2. C.H. Spurgeon, *An All Round Ministry*, The Banner of Truth Trust, first published 1900, this edition 1972, p. ix.
3. Dietrich Bonhoeffer, *The Cost of Discipleship*, SCM Press, first published 1937, this edition 2001, *The Memoirs*, p. xvi. See also Eric Metaxas, *Bonhoeffer*, Thomas Nelson, 2010, chapter 18.
4. Bonhoeffer, *The Cost of Discipleship*, p. 44.
5. Dr & Mrs Howard Taylor, *Hudson Taylor and the China Inland Mission*, R&R Clark, first published 1918, p. 621.
6. Dr and Mrs Howard Taylor, *Hudson Taylor in Early Years*, R&R Clark, first published 1911, 1930, p. 126.
7. Dietrich Bonhoeffer, *Life Together*, SCM Press, 9th edition, 1972, p. 22.
8. Ibid.

Chapter 2. He Called Them to His Words

1. John Calvin, *Institutes of the Christian Religion*, The Library of Christian Classics, vol 20, The Westminster Press, 1975, 3/2/6.

Chapter 3. He Called Them Each by Name

1. J. Oswald Sanders, *Problems of Christian Discipleship*, OMF Books, London, p. 113.

2. Bonhoeffer, *Life Together*, p. 7.

3. Miriam Huffman Rockness, *A Passion for the Impossible*, Discovery House, 2015, p. 86.

Chapter 4. He Calls Them Through the Testimony of His People

1. John Murray, *Collected Writings*, The Banner of Truth Trust, Volume 1, chapter 33, The Church and Mission, pp. 251, 252. In commenting here on Acts 8:4 Murray says, 'If there is the universal priesthood, there is also the universal prophethood. And herein lies the mission of the church.'

2. D.A. Carson, *The Gospel According to John*, Apollos, 1991, p. 159. See also his remarks on pp. 91,481,482 on the overall purpose of John's Gospel account.

3. Iain Murray, *Evangelicalism Divided*, The Banner of Truth Trust, 2000, p. 1.

4. G. Taylor, *Pastor Hsi*, Christian Focus, 2005, p. 83.

5. A. Bonar, *Memoir and Remains of R.M. M'Cheyne*, The Banner of Truth, Trust, first published 1844, 1960, p. 48.

6. Taylor, *Pastor Hsi*, p. 86.

Chapter 5. He Trains Them Within the Church

1. E.M. Bounds, *Power Through Prayer*, Moody Press, 1979, p. 14.

Chapter 6. As Loved Apprentices in the Church

1. John Bunyan, *Prayer*, The Banner of Truth Trust, first published 1662, this edition 1965, p. 38.
2. C.H. Spurgeon, *The Early Years*, The Banner of Truth Trust, volume 1, p. 182.

Chapter 7. The Disciple-Maker's Goals for the Disciple

1. S. Ferguson, *The Whole Christ*, Crossway, 2016, p. 52.

Chapter 8. Examples of Disciple-Making

1. Thomas Hardy, *Under the Greenwood Tree*, 1960, Macmillan, p. 11.
2. Jun'ichirō Tanizaki, *In Praise of Shadows*, Vintage Books, 2001, for an architect's view of the worth of shadows.

Chapter 9. The Challege

1. Bonhoeffer, *The Cost of Discipleship*, p. 45.
2. Taylor, *Hudson Taylor in Early Years*, p. 365.

Acknowledgements

A big thank you to my wife Cathy, my children, West Church members and friends for encouraging me while writing this book.

Resources

The following is a list of books that I have found to be particularly helpful and relevant to the topic of disciple-making.

A.B. Bruce	*The Training of the Twelve*, first published 1871, multiple publishers and editions.
T. Boston	*The Art of Man Fishing*, first published 1773, Christian Heritage, 2012.
S. Olyott	*Ministering Like the Master*, Banner of Truth, 2017.
T.K. Ascol (ed)	*Dear Timothy*, Founders Press, 2004, chapter 17, 'Train other Men', Steve Martin.
L. Eims	*The Lost Art of Disciple Making*, Zondervan, 1978. *Winning Ways*, Victor Books, 1974.
D. Bonhoeffer	*Life Together*, first published 1939, HarperOne 1978. *The Cost of Discipleship*, first published 1937, Touchstone, 1995.
W.A. Henrichsen	*Disciples are Made Not Born*, first published 1974, David C. Cook, 2011.

About the Author

Stephen J. Turner was born in New Zealand, was brought up on a dairy farm, and is part of an extended family in which the Gospel has been honoured for generations.

He has been married for forty years and has seven children and eight grandchildren.

He began his public ministry of the Word in 1973 and since then has continued investing his life in preaching and teaching the Gospel, and in giving his own life in disciple-making.

www.ingramcontent.com/pod-product-compliance
Lightning Source LLC
Chambersburg PA
CBHW062052290426
44109CB00027B/2799